CIPS Stu

Level 4

Foundation Diploma in Purchasing and Supply

PASSNOTES

Measuring Purchasing Performance

Printed and distributed by the Chartered Institute of Purchasing & Supply
Easton House, Easton on the Hill, Stamford, Lincolnshire PE9 3NZ
Tel: +44 (0) 1780 756 777
Fax: +44 (0) 1780 751 610
Email: info@cips.org
Website: www.cips.org

First edition July 2006
Second edition April 2009
Reprinted with minor amendments October 2010

Contents

Preface

Welcome to your **Passnotes**!

This element of your Study Pack has been specially designed to support you in your exam revision.

- Small-format **Passnotes** fit easily into a bag or briefcase: **convenient to use** wherever and whenever you have a few minutes for topic review or exam revision.
- The material is organised in **short, clearly labelled units**: easy to work through systematically or to dip into at any point, if that's what you prefer.
- Each area of the unit content starts with a simple **mind-map** of the relevant Learning Objectives, helpfully **cross-referenced** to chapters in your Course Book (so you can quickly locate more substantial topic coverage, if you need to refresh your memory).
- The units cover each (and all) of the **Learning Objectives** in turn (again, cross-referenced to other units where topics overlap), so you can see exactly what knowledge and understanding underpins potential exam questions.
- Within each unit, the material is presented in a format specially designed for **ease and speed of learning** – essential in the revision stage of your studies! **Passnotes** use key definitions, point lists, action plans, tables and diagrams:
  - To keep the topic coverage as focused and brief as possible
  - To offer an easily grasped overview of each topic
  - To make the topic more visual – and therefore (for most people) more readily memorable.
- For relevant topics, we also include Integrated Learning Checklists: point lists and action plans gathered from different Learning Objectives to give you a broader handle on topics, processes and management challenges. (Particularly useful for case study questions…)

Of course, Passnotes don't give you substantial or comprehensive coverage of the unit content. (That's what your **Course Book** is for.) What they do give you is **systematic and focused coverage**: a concise, easy-to-remember survey of the key points on which you can base an exam answer. This makes them ideal to use in the weeks and days leading up to the exam!

And don't forget: updates, case studies, advice on exam technique and other revision-support resources (including practice questions with full solutions) will be regularly added to the study resources.

Good luck.

Learning Objective 1.0: Measuring the performance of the purchasing and supply function

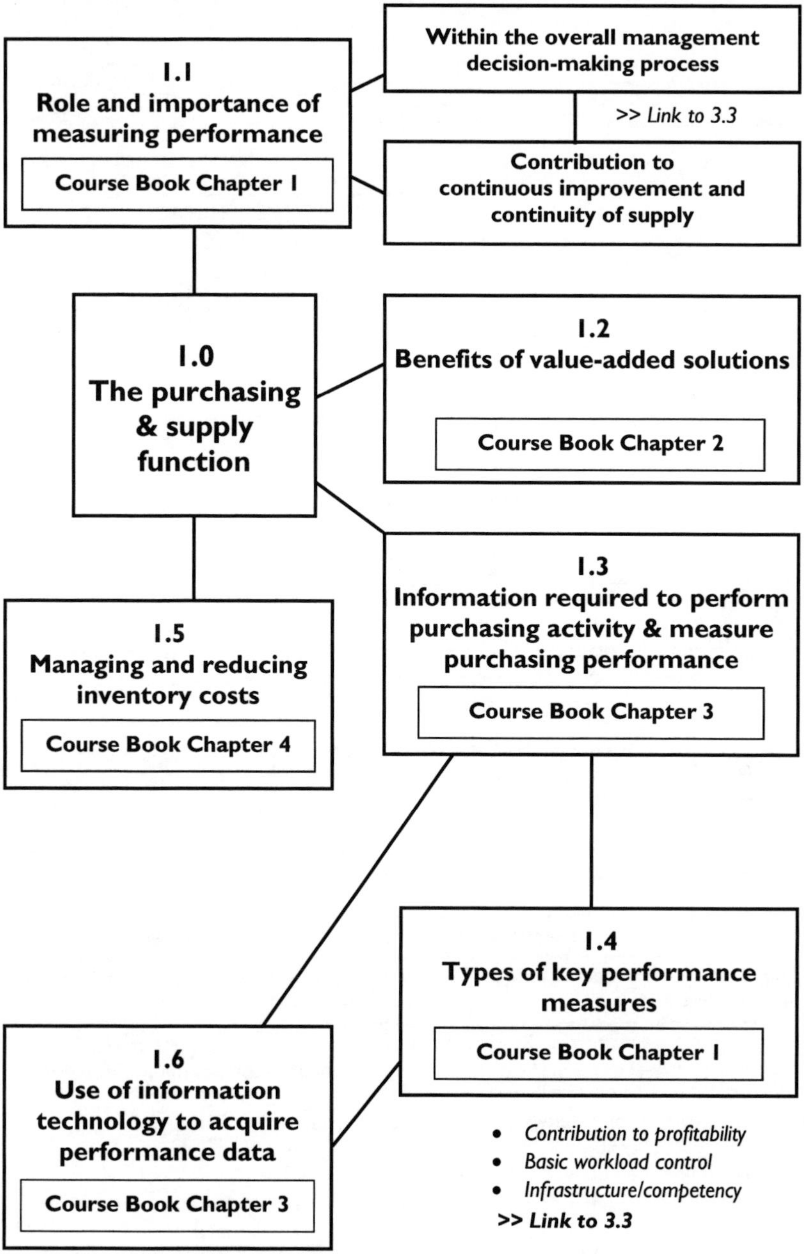

1.1 Evaluate the role and importance of measuring performance

Performance measurement as a control tool

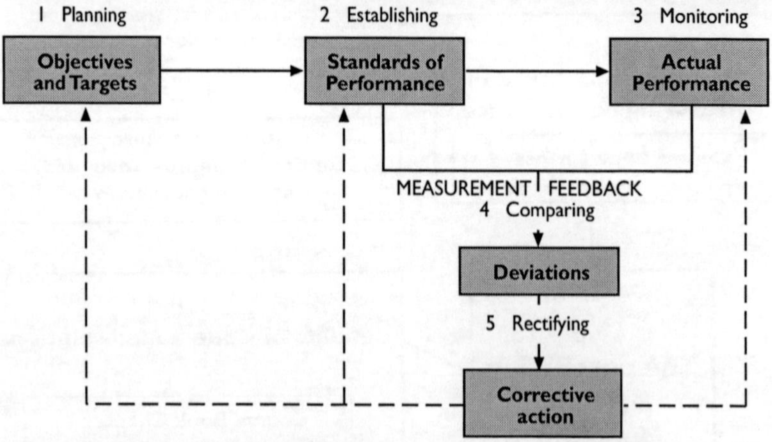

- ❑ Controlled performance > satisfy legitimate expectations of **stakeholders**
- ❑ 'What gets measured, gets **managed**'
- ❑ Measuring purchasing performance > measuring **supply chain** performance

Supply chain management (SCM) is 'the management of relations and integrated business processes across the supply chain… Use of the SCM concept entails that the links in the supply chain plan and co-ordinate their processes and relationships by weighing the overall efficiency and competitive power of the supply chain.' *(Jespersen & Skjøtt-Larsen)*

Advantages and disadvantages of performance measurement

Advantages	**Disadvantages**
Aids business planning and control of operations	Design/establishment of system is a complex task
Can lead to performance improvement	Takes time, money and effort to operate
Important tool for communicating with stakeholders	Too many KPIs can lead to information overload
Key performance indicators (KPIs) can motivate individual managers/teams	Pursuit of individual KPIs can lead to dysfunctional or sub-optimising behaviour

- ☒ Cutting corners on quality/service to achieve productivity/time targets
- ☒ Price/profitability cuts to achieve volume sales targets
- ☒ Price competition between branches/departments/teams
- ☒ Focus on own targets at expense of cross-functional collaboration, co-ordination

>> Need to integrate performance measures with overall organisational goals

Link to mission and strategic goals/objectives

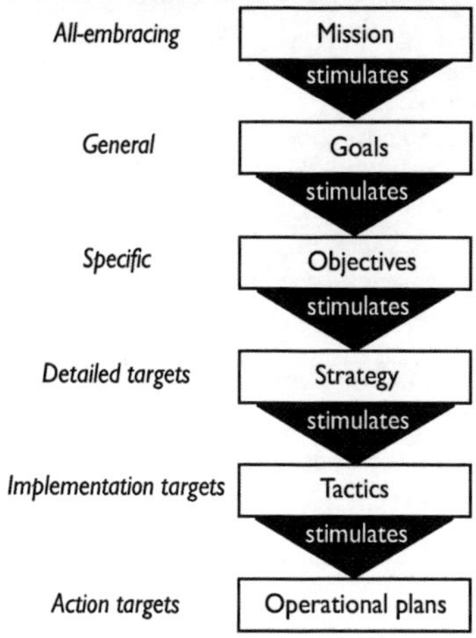

Mission statement describes purpose, business area and key values, in qualitative terms.

Goals: desired future state ('where we want to get to')

Objectives: specific targets to pursue ('what we need to do to get there')

Strategic plans apply to whole organisation, focusing on the broad direction over long term (3-5 years)

Tactical plans apply to particular divisions and functions, focusing on tasks required to pursue strategies in particular markets, over medium term (1-2 years)

Operational plans apply to departments and units, focusing on detailed activity, targets, resources, over short term (up to 1 year)

>> **Vertical alignment:** ensure that all sub-unit efforts contribute to overall corporate mission, for unity of direction

>> **Horizontal alignment:** ensure that efforts of different sub-units dovetail with each other, for co-ordinated effort and a coherent face to the world

Corporate strategy — What businesses the firm should be involved in and how these are integrated with each other

↓

Business strategy — How each SBU (division or subsidiary) should attempt to achieve its objectives

↓

Functional strategy — How function can best support business/corporate strategy

eg

Corporate objectives	Purchasing objectives
Maintain/increase market share	Provide supplies to match customer needs; assure quality; reduce delivery lead times; reduce costs
Improve profits, cash flow, return on capital	Reduce/control stocks; improve reliability; more frequent deliveries
Eliminate non-core activities	Effective make-or-buy policies; integrate purchasing and capacity planning
Introduce continuous improvement	Reduce/control supplier base; develop partnership relationships; improve processes and systems; improve communications along the supply chain

1.1 Evaluate the role and importance of measuring performance

Developing effective performance measures *(Neely et al)*

❑ **Truth**	Are we really measuring what we set out to measure?
❑ **Focus**	Are we measuring only what we set out to measure?
❑ **Relevance**	Are we definitely measuring the right thing?
❑ **Consistency**	Does it give the same result whenever and by whomever done?
❑ **Accessibility**	Can the data be easily accessed and understood?
❑ **Clarity**	Are the results free from ambiguity in interpretation?
❑ **'So what?'**	Will the result be acted upon?
❑ **Timeliness**	Is the data available in time to affect action?
❑ **Cost**	How much does the measurement cost to perform?
❑ **'Gaming'**	What behaviour(s) will the measurement encourage?

Effective measures *(CIPS)*
Reliable
Meaningful
Focused on core issues/success factors
Fair and balanced (strengths/weaknesses)
Capable of change and improvement
'Manage the target' (ie improve output)

eg Purchasing areas for measurement
Identifying and evaluating suppliers
Awarding contracts and/or placing orders
Managing relationships with suppliers
Managing tenders
Managing data input
Managing the supplier base

Contribution to purchasing management objectives

Contribution of performance measurement to P & S goals

Cost management

- Measure effectiveness and efficiency of funds management
- Highlight areas for cost saving or need for tighter control
- P & S measures eg cost savings/reductions, contribution to profit, conformance with budget
- Supplier measures eg liquidity, efficiency, cost structure

Continuous improvement

- Measures > feedback on performance, highlight areas for improvement
- Quality measures > defect prevention/reduction
- People measures > identify learning and development needs
- *Hansei kaizen:* continuous self-reflection, measurement and incremental adjustment

Continuity of supply

- Measures to highlight supply risks: eg cost of stockouts, cost of holding buffer stocks, production hold-ups due to stockouts + measures of supplier capability, reliability, performance
- Supports risk management via: multiple (back-up) sources of supply, supplier performance management, partnership with key suppliers, buffer stocks etc

Kaizen (continuous improvement) 'is both a rigorous, scientific method of using statistical quality control and a framework of organisational values and beliefs that keep management and workers focused on zero defects'.

Plan	Implement (small scale)	Measure	Evaluate results/process > identify learning

Explain the benefits of value-added solutions 1.2

Value is the 'worth' of a product or service: what it costs the organisation to produce and what the customer is willing to pay for it. **Value added** is a measure of the value added to a product, for its customers, by the various processes that support its production and supply.

Porter: added value is ultimately measured by the amount customers are willing to pay for products/services *above* the cost to the firm of carrying out all its value-creating activities:

Added value = total revenue *minus* **total costs** of all activities undertaken to develop and market the product/service.

Value-adding solutions are therefore based on:

❑ Providing additional product/service attributes to attract a premium price OR
❑ Reducing production/process costs > provide equivalent product at lower prices.

The value chain

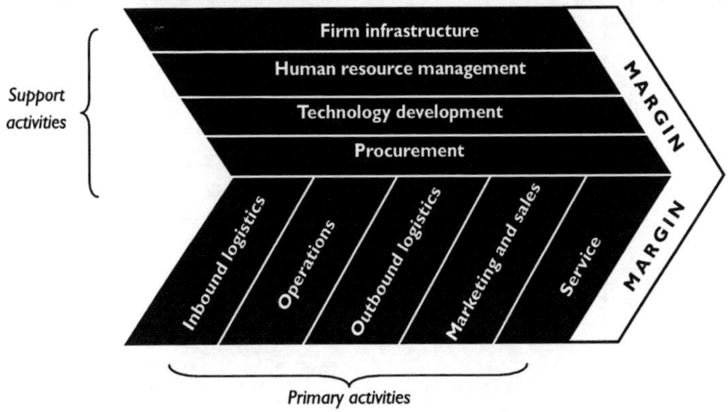

Porter

- 'Each activity within the value chain provides inputs which, after processing, constitute added value to the output received by the ultimate customer.' *(Lysons & Farrington)*
- Activities within the value chain are interdependent: each element can affect the costs/effectiveness of another, via 'linkages': these require co-ordination in order to optimise the flow of value.

The **value system** is the wider network of value-adding activities and linkages extended through the supply chain.

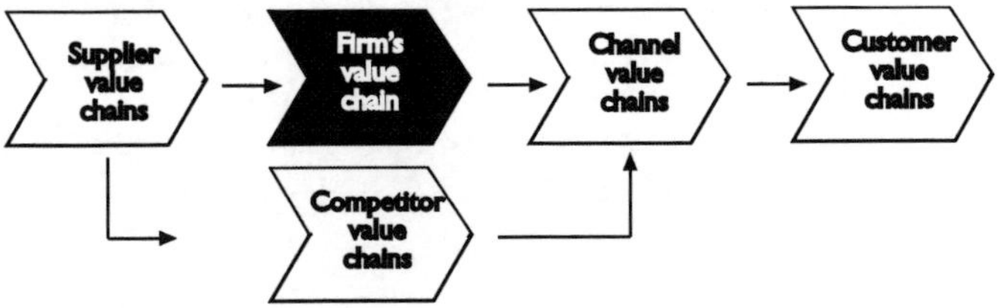

1.2 Explain the benefits of value-added solutions

Purchasing contribution to added value

'Make it faster, move it faster, get paid faster' *(Emmett)*

Measures of purchasing efficiency *(Focus on minimising inputs)*	**Measures of purchasing effectiveness** *(Focus on enhancing outputs)*
Basic purchase price of inputs	Quality of output
Cost of placing an order	Quality of service to customers
Cost of staffing the purchasing function	Achieving objectives within budget
Speed of transaction processing	Quality of supplier relationships
Use of information technology	Impact on profitability
Efficiency of organisational structure	Prompt delivery to customers
Efficiency of supplier management	

Value-added solutions

Cost savings from improved performance

- ❑ Effective negotiation and/or tendering, aggregated orders etc > reduced materials costs
- ❑ User dialogue > improved specifications, demand management
- ❑ Supplier + quality management > reduced errors/wastage
- ❑ Supplier relationships > cost/price advantages (competitive) or working together to reduce costs (collaborative)
- ❑ Measure 'total cost of ownership' (TOC) – not just 'price'.

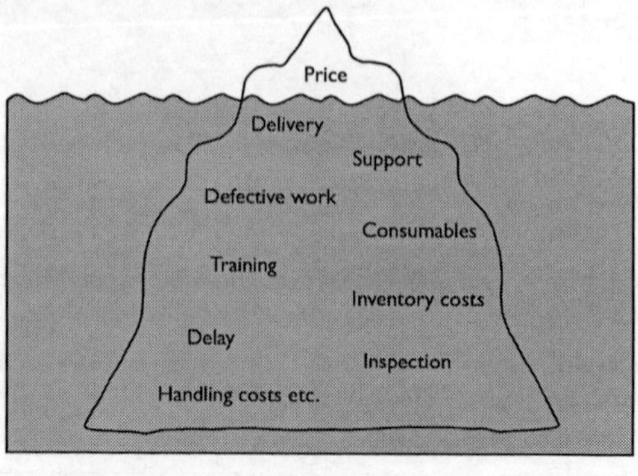

Eg: thinking through effects of:

- Price savings at expense of quality (> added quality costs)
- Discounts for bulk purchase (> added stockholding costs)
- Purchasing objectives (eg cost savings) v user/organisational objectives (eg quality, flexibility, speed)

- ❑ Whole life (lifecycle) costing approach to purchase of capital assets > maximise total benefits in relationship to total costs.

Explain the benefits of value-added solutions 1.2

Reducing inventory costs

[>> Unit 1.5]

- ❑ Demand management > reduce surplus-to-requirement stocks
- ❑ Maintain buffer/safety stocks (to avoid cost of stockouts) – but at minimum levels (to avoid unnecessary inventory cost)
- ❑ Effective inventory management > minimise costs of acquiring and holding stock + loss of value through obsolescence, deterioration or pilferage etc
- ❑ Just in time (JIT) purchasing: close co-ordination with suppliers to deliver as demand arises (not before)

Target costing

Traditional pricing: costs + profit margin = selling price

Target costing: estimated selling price market will accept *minus* acceptable profit margin = target costs

- ☑ Requires focus on cost reduction and control
- ☑ Views value from point of view of market/consumer
- ☑ Requires trust eg open book costing (cost transparency by supplier) > closer collaboration, joint value-adding solutions

Contract terms: extended payment and warranty

Extended payment terms = longer period to pay. Purchase price remains in buyer's bank account, earning interest on deposit, reducing loan interest – but can damage buyer/supplier relations if exploited!

Warranty terms: supplier is liable to compensate buyer for costs/losses incurred as a result of supplier failure (eg errors/defects leading to disrupted operations or customer complaint).

Using consignment stock

Suppliers provide a buyer with stock, on the buyer's premises, but without charging for it in advance: buyer pays for stock as used.

- ☑ Protects buyer's cashflow and transfers risk/cost to supplier
- ☑ Allows safety/buffer stock – at minimal expense to buyer
- ☑ Supplier benefits from preferred supplier status, supply planning (little impact from demand fluctuation)

Improving organisational efficiency

- ❑ Effective functional management of purchasing > reduced contracting and transaction costs
- ❑ Centralising (> savings from aggregated orders, bargaining leverage) or decentralising (> reduced transport/storage costs)
- ❑ Outsourcing or off-shoring non-core competencies > obtain value at less cost, focus resources more efficiently
- ❑ Applying ICT and automation > streamline processes (eg e-procurement); increase productivity; support planning etc.
- ❑ Eliminate waste throughout the supply chain eg by value analysis and engineering, process (re)engineering, collaboration to eliminate process inefficiencies and costs > 'lean' supply

1.3 Identify and explain the information required to perform purchasing activities and how to measure purchasing performance

Purchasing goals and objectives

- ❑ What objectives and targets the purchasing function is attempting to meet (for comparison against performance > extent to which they are achieved)
- ❑ The strategic goals of the organisation – and how purchasing objectives contribute to their fulfilment *[**>> Unit 1.1**]*
- ❑ Potential areas of conflict with organisational and/or other functional objectives > agreed trade-offs (cost, quality, delivery etc) according to organisational priorities
- ❑ Purchasing performance measures increasingly integrated with business measures (eg re profitability, quality, corporate social responsibility, ethics)

Product/service specifications

Specification communicates **buyer's needs** to supplier + establishes **criteria** by which to judge what is delivered >> purchasers need info on **user requirements**:

- Design considerations: functionality
- Marketing considerations: consumer acceptance
- Manufacturing considerations: economical production
- Procurement considerations: markets, materials availability, supplier capabilities, cost

Performance (or functional) specification

Describes what product/material should achieve: **functions** performed and **level** of performance.

☑ Little technical knowledge required; supplier bears responsibility for performance; widens potential supplier base

Conformance (or design) specification

Details exactly what required product/material must **consist of**.

☒ Difficult to draft exact description; buyer bears risk of poor specification (as long as goods conform, supplier protected); restricted potential for innovative solutions

Effective specification

- Up-to-date (latest design decisions and supplier materials)
- Detailed technical description (with copy of design or sample)
- Estimate of materials and packaging requirements

Specification of products/materials
Performance (basic operating)
Perceived quality (brand, reputation etc)
Features (optional extras)
Conformance (key criteria/standards on which item must meet buyer's needs)
Reliability (rate of repair/maintenance)
Serviceability (ease of maintenance)
Aesthetics (pleasing appearance)
Durability (length of useful life)

Specification of services *(Parasuraman)*
Reliability of service
Competence (skill and knowledge of staff)
Courtesy (of supplier staff)
Understanding (supplier attempt to understand customer requirements)
Tangibles (physical goods as part of service)
Security (management of customer risk)
Credibility (supplier trustworthiness)
Access (how easy it is to contact supplier)
Responsiveness (prompt/willing service)

***Advantages* of specifications**
Useful discipline > careful consideration of needs and options > cost savings
Multiple sourcing: use of conformance specs ensures uniformity
Useful criteria for measuring quality and acceptability of items once delivered
Clarifies accountability for performance

***Limitations* of specifications**
Expensive process (uneconomic for small value purchases)
Higher costs of inspection/testing than if eg purchasing by known brand name, sample
Specs can become too firmly embedded: need for regular review, flexibility

Resource requirements

- Resources required by user departments > purchasing responsibility for supplying (performance measured on 'five rights' of purchasing).
- User requirements communicated via specifications, purchase requisitions from users and/or stock replenishment triggered by inventory levels etc.
- NB: future resource requirements (of strategic goals) > advance process and supplier development, purchasing research etc.
- Resources required by purchasing department itself > purchasing responsibility for efficient and effective use, conformance with budget etc.

Cost/price information

- Total costs of ownership (or whole life costs of capital items) > support investment and management decisions (eg repair or replace)
- Sourcing/purchasing/materials costs > support cost management and reduction
- Prices in the supply market ('market price'), factors affecting price, pricing methods
- Prices charged by particular suppliers and vendors > comparison of suppliers, purchase cost estimation and budgeting, supplier negotiation and so on
- Supplier cost structure > support comparison of supplier prices, evaluation of supplier prices and proposed price increases, assessment of potential for price negotiation/reduction.
  - **Cost behaviour**: way in which costs of output are (variable costs) or are not (fixed costs) affected by fluctuations in level of activity
  - **Contribution** (towards covering fixed costs and making a profit): selling price *minus* variable cost of the goods sold. A certain level of sales will cover fixed costs (breakeven point) and thereafter earn a profit.
  - **Costing method**: marginal costing (of producing additional units: ie variable costs only) or absorption costing (proportion of fixed costs also added).
  - **Profit** expressed as a percentage of cost ('mark-up') or as a percentage of selling price ('margin) > check that supplier is not earning 'excessive' levels of profit.

1.3 Identify and explain the information required to perform purchasing activities and how to measure purchasing performance

Inventory information

- ❑ Availability of items in stock: ie current stock balances + estimates/monitoring of demand, productivity and utilisation rates > forecast replenishment needs, level of safety stocks, economic order quantities etc.
- ❑ Stock movements (into, through and out of storage system) to maintain control of stock balances and locations
- ❑ Info re special storage requirements (eg refrigeration) + damage, loss, deterioration of items in stock > plan security, insurance, stock rotation, health & safety issues etc

[>> Unit 1.5, 1.6]

Supplier/vendor information

- ❑ Info about suppliers (potential suppliers) and vendors (current suppliers) for purposes of supplier selection/evaluation and performance measurement/management.
- ❑ Sources of supplier info: formal search/request; own past experience and records; other customers; network contacts (other buyers); supplier sales force and promotions; supplier audits (on-site visits and surveys); online directories and supplier websites; published catalogues; trade directories, journals and exhibitions.

[>> Unit 2.1 – 2.4]

Supply market information

- ❑ Suppliers within the market, degree of product differentiation, methods of pricing
- ❑ Structure of the market: number of buyers/suppliers, relative bargaining power/dominance of buyers/suppliers etc
- ❑ Environmental factors (PESTLE: Political, Economic, Socio-cultural, Technological, Legal, Ecological) that may affect continuity or price of supply – eg: scarcity of natural resources; vulnerability to weather/terrorism/industrial action; fluctuating foreign exchange rates affecting prices; new protections for intellectual property; import quotas and tariffs; consumer values (eg re sustainability, ethical/'green' issues)
- ❑ Sources of info: supplier/vendor consultation; historical trends; published indices (eg price); economic models; specialist forecasting agencies.

Purchasing research

Ongoing research (and/or defined research projects) into supply markets: to provide info so firm can plan to adapt to changes in supply environment + to secure competitive advantage by early info on opportunities, innovations

Demand analysis	**Vendor analysis**	**Market analysis**
Likely usage of materials in period ahead (> priority focus on high-value, high-usage.)	Performance of potential + current suppliers Optimum type of buying agreement	Structure of market Likely availability/ shortages, prices and price fluctuations of materials

Analyse the types and categories of key performance measures available to organisations — 1.4

Contribution to profitability

- ❑ Sourcing strategies > reduce materials, transaction, quality, stock holding costs
- ❑ Reduction in production costs/inefficiencies eg via materials planning, JIT supply, quality management, effective specification, own process efficiencies
- ❑ Contribution to make/do or buy decisions > outsource support activities
- ❑ Contribution to value analysis and value engineering > waste reduction
- ❑ Supplier relations > price leverage (competitive), joint cost reduction (collaborative)
- ❑ Applied ICT/automation > streamline processes (eg EDI), reduce overheads (eg virtual teams), lower prices (eg e-auctions) etc.
- ❑ Profitability not solely based on price: need to consider total cost of ownership >> impact on profitability via long-term decisions re quality, supply reliability etc.
- ❑ Need to balance price with non-price criteria (eg quality, environment, ethics)

Profitability is primary responsibility, although organisations also have secondary goals and responsibilities (important for *sustainable* profitability and stakeholder satisfaction).

Contribution to quality and continuous improvement objectives

- ❑ Product development: early involvement; value engineering; materials specification
- ❑ Supplier selection and appraisal: eg approved supplier lists, certification
- ❑ Contract management eg mutual understanding of standards, incentives/penalties etc
- ❑ Monitoring and managing quality and timely delivery of incoming supplies
- ❑ Supplier relations > collaborative quality management, continuous improvement
- ❑ Measurement, evaluation and improvement of supplier performance eg vendor rating

Contribution to corporate social responsibility (CSR) objectives

- ❑ Draw up and enforce codes of practice for ethical sourcing
- ❑ Adhere to CIPS ethical code and Ethical Trading Initiative principles
- ❑ Encourage/enforce ethical employment/environmental practices in suppliers
- ❑ Adhere to health and safety, equal opportunity and ethical employment practices

Basic workload control

P & S function measured on effectiveness and efficiency of purchasing activity/processes.

☑ Materials of the	**Right QUALITY**	
☑ Are delivered in the	**Right QUANTITY**	
☑ At the	**Right PLACE**	[From the **Right SOURCE**]
☑ At the	**Right TIME**	
☑ For the	**Right PRICE**	

Supported by:

- ❑ Development of purchasing policies/procedures manuals
- ❑ Statement of purchasing policies and ethics within the overall corporate plan
- ❑ Appropriate training in 'Five Rights' of purchasing
- ❑ Appropriate training in bid evaluation and contract award criteria
- ❑ Development of suitable ICT systems to support efficient processes

1.4 Analyse the types and categories of key performance measures available to organisations

Efficiency measures	eg
Cost	Procurement costs as a % of spend
Staffing	Staff per £million of spend (or labour cost per employee)
Productivity	Purchase orders/material receipts per employee (or per period) Cost per purchase order/receipt
Technology leverage	Technology cost as a % of procurement cost % of purchase orders (etc) communicated electronically
Cycle time	Hours required to complete a requisition and purchase order
Standardisation	Use of company-wide policies, commodity codes

Effectiveness measures	eg
Cost savings/ control	Annual cost savings as a % of spend Price movements over time
Supplier leverage	% of suppliers providing 80% or more of annual spend % of purchases made from preferred suppliers
Error rates	% of transactions requiring correction after process
Customer satisfaction	% of deliveries received in full and on time (IFOT)
Strategic alignment	Visibility of a formal documented procurement strategy % of objectives linked to business strategy

Performance measures used depend on the role of the purchasing function *(Van Weele)*:

- If primarily administrative, measures eg lead times, productivity and error rates
- If primarily commercial, cost savings will be a priority.
- If strategic, higher measures eg strategic alignment, supplier leverage etc

Development of purchasing infrastructure

P & S function measured on efficiency and effectiveness of structures and systems. Eg:

❑ **Integration of information systems** *(Syson; Minkema)*

Independence ↓	Purchasing operates to own guidelines > sub-optimisation. Standalone system > operational decisions, computations
Dependence ↓	Dovetailing with other functions via consultation, reporting. Standalone system > operational decisions, data processing
Business integration ↓	Systematic integration with other functions > internal co-ordination (eg supporting MRP)
Chain integration	Systematic co-operation along supply chain > internal/external co-ordination (eg supporting JIT)

❑ **Efficiency of purchasing structure** eg part-centralised (coordination, standardisation, economies of scale) and part local (responsiveness, shorter supply lines, managerial accountability for performance)

❑ **Scope/integration of purchasing responsibilities** eg towards integrated materials management, logistics or supply chain management approach

- **Effectiveness of structural relationships** with internal customers and collaborators eg use of cross-functional project structures, CLAN/lead-buyer structures, use of expertise/influence in relationships with line departments etc
- **Effectiveness of network relationships** with suppliers, 'external operations' (outsource providers), strategic alliances/partnerships

Development of purchasing competency

P & S function measured on ability to secure, retain and develop people with knowledge and skills to meet current and future challenges.

- Staff competence in defined purchasing disciplines and tasks
- Staff development for trends in purchasing role > external operations (outsourcing) management, cross-functional projects, supplier network relationships, strategic awareness etc
- Ongoing staff training and development for continuous learning and improvement
- Knowledge management: ensuring that information and learning is shared and retained
- Best practice sharing: benchmarking, quality circles, professional networking etc > promote best practice
- Support for purchasing professionalism (eg CIPS qualification and continuing professional development)

Developing key performance indicators (KPIs)

Key performance indicators are agreed, quantifiable measures of the performance of a unit or organisation in relation to its critical success factors.

Identify critical success factors ↓	Areas of key competitive advantage, or factors necessary for success
Determine measures of success or improvement for each factor/area ↓	Balance quantitative (cost/quantity) & qualitative (subjective/quality) measures
Develop KPIs with key stakeholders ↓	Eg involve users, finance, marketing, suppliers
Agree KPIs with key stakeholders ↓	Ensure KPIs are: ☑ Relevant ☑ Clear and unambiguous ☑ Capable of direct, detailed and consistent measurement at operational level (using available data collection systems) ☑ Backed up by incentives/penalties *and* contingency plans (in event of failure)
Communicate KPIs to stakeholders	

1.5 Analyse and explain the methods that an organisation can use to manage and reduce inventory costs

Reasons for holding inventory

Advantages of holding stock	*Disadvantages of holding stock*
Safety stock: minimise risk/cost of stockouts (from disrupted production, peak demand, long delivery lead-times)	Opportunity costs of working capital committed, loss of interest on capital tied up in stock
Maintain service levels, availability/response	Reduced flexibility to change of spec
Reduced *acquisition* costs: economies of scale (eg bulk discount, fewer orders); advance purchase to manage fluctuations in commodity prices, exchange rates	Increased *holding* costs: insurance, warehouse/stores space, staff, handling equipment etc
Finished-item stock to anticipate cyclical peaks in demand	Risk of deterioration, damage, pilfering, obsolescence while in stock

Stock control is 'the systematic regulation of stock levels with respect to time and quantity.' (*BS5191*) The objective of a **stock control system** is to minimise stockholding while meeting target service levels.

- Monitor the movement of materials/goods in and out of stores
- Indicate re-order points and quantities
- Prioritise by value/usage (ABC analysis) for stock segregation and management
- Maintain sufficient stock to provide required service to users
- Ensure that stock movements are appropriately documented and controlled
- Minimise total costs of inventory consistent with the above

Costs of inventory

Costs of acquiring stock

- Costs of setting up and maintaining transaction processing systems and staff
- Requisition/ordering/delivery/payment costs > favours large orders (trade off with stock holding costs > favours small orders)
- Purchase price of stock

Costs of holding stock

- Warehouse/stores costs: staff, building and site, equipment, services
- Packing materials/consumables
- Maintenance and repair
- Opportunity cost of capital tied up in inventory
- Insurance costs
- Loss of value through deterioration, pilferage, damage, obsolescence etc

(May be classified as costs of receipt, inspection, putting stock away, holding stock in store, picking stock for internal/external customers, packaging stock and despatch)

Analyse and explain the methods that an organisation can use to manage and reduce inventory costs 1.5

Inventory management approaches

>> **Purchasing for production**: buying for immediate incorporation into manufacturing process. Feature of:

- ❑ Capital project sectors (eg construction): purchase for needs of each project stage
- ❑ Just in time (JIT) environments: minimising or eliminating 'buffer' stock: materials purchased just before required in production process. (Requires close collaboration between buyer/supplier to anticipate demand, minimise lead times.)

JIT is a Japanese management philosophy which 'provides for the cost-effective production and delivery of only the necessary quantity of parts at the right quantity, at the right time and place, while using the minimum amount of facilities, equipment, materials and human resources.' (*Voss*)

METHODS OF MINIMISING STOCK-HOLDING:

- ❑ Review/audit regularly to ensure levels meet current and forecast requirements
- ❑ Review criticality of items (eg using Pareto/ABC analysis) and supply risks/lead times: reduce or eliminate safety stock of non-critical, readily/reliably sourced items
- ❑ Improve accuracy of demand forecasting (eg work more closely with Sales, EPOS information)
- ❑ Undertake variety reduction/standardisation to enable shorter lead times, substitution
- ❑ Use economic order quantities (calculate optimum order size for minimum cost of acquiring *and* holding stocks)
- ❑ Improve inventory control (eg by using MRP systems)
- ❑ Use vendor-managed inventory (get supplier to hold/manage stock)

Fixed order quantity	When stock falls to a predetermined level, replenished with a predetermined quantity (eg based on **economic order quantity** model: holding/acquisition cost balance > show level at which lowest total costs obtained).
ABC analysis	Pareto: 80% of total value of material accounted for by 20% of items > categorise stock items: small number, high usage/value (Category A); medium number/usage/value (Category B); high number, low usage/value (Category C) >> strategic/operational priorities (inventory and quality management etc).
Materials requirements planning	A set of logically related procedures, decision rules and documents designed to translate customers orders and demand forecasts into production schedules and time-phased net materials requirements. ☑ Focus on customer needs ☑ Flexible response to demand variations ☑ Accurate materials planning > reduced inventory levels

1.5 Analyse and explain the methods that an organisation can use to manage and reduce inventory costs

KPIs for inventory management

- ❑ **Total cost of holding stock as % of stock value** (eg average costs of goods in stock at any point in year; cost of total goods issued to customers during year) – ideally, low ratio. Can be compared between periods to show improvement/deterioration
- ❑ **Stock turnover ratio**: speed with which stock moves through system (slow = idle stock).

Stock turnover ratio (1)	Number of times per year stock is turned over (v. cost of sales) $\frac{\text{Cost of sales}}{\text{Average (or closing) stock}}$ = times/yr	Monitor ratio from one period to next: too much stock held (doesn't turn over often)? NB consider nature of business…
Stock turnover ratio (2)	Number of days for which stock held is (on average) sufficient. $\frac{\text{Average stock during yr}}{\text{Cost of sales}} \times 365$	Monitor ratio from one period to next: too much stock held (lasts too long)? NB consider nature of business…

- ❑ **Economy:** achieving best value for money from stock costs
- ❑ **Efficiency:** use of appropriate inventory management systems/techniques > meet objectives without waste of inputs
- ❑ **Effectiveness:** satisfactory level of service provided by inventory function to end users

Measures of economy	***Measures of efficiency***	***Measures of effectiveness***
Purchase cost of input items	Number of stock items held	Service level achieved
Cost of stock losses (eg through obsolescence)	Quantity held of each stock item	Cost of stock losses (eg through obsolescence, damage)
Cost of stores staff	Rapidity of stock turnover	Rapidity of stock turnover
Average value of stock held	Average period each item held in stock	% orders completed on-time, in-full (OTIF)
Cost of stores operations	Speed of stock picking	Customer returns/ complaints
	Outstanding back orders	Health and safety compliance

NB: depending on the product/service being procured, there may be other appropriate KPIs including: legal compliance (eg with health and safety or transport of hazardous goods regulations); environmental responsibility (eg target waste/emissions, % recyclable, cost of disassembly/disposal); sustainability (eg % sourced from local suppliers) and so on.

Analyse and explain how the use of information technology may help in the acquisition of P & S performance data 1.6

Information technology for performance measurement

☑ Automated capture, storage and integration of transaction/performance data from multiple sources eg in a database system
☑ Automated (fair, objective) comparison of performance with plan (order, budget, specification, KPIs etc) + comparison of suppliers, tenders etc
☑ High speed, flexible processing of data > user needs (trend analysis, comparisons etc)
☑ Reporting by exception eg triggered by variances or need for authorisation
☑ Automated action to decision parameters (eg purchase at defined stock level/price)
☑ Enhanced monitoring and control eg order/delivery tracking and expediting

Eg access to real-time reports on:

- Details of purchase orders (items ordered, supplier details, value etc)
- Delivery schedules and backorders awaiting delivery
- Goods received and quality records (eg details of % rejects per supplier)
- Cost per order raised, or spend per buyer or per category of goods
- Cost savings and/or added value

Management information systems (MIS)

Management information systems (MIS) are systems that take information captured by transaction processing systems (eg EPOS) and produce reports to support managerial planning and control.

Hardware	Software	People/users	Communication links	Data

❑ Sales, purchase, investment, payroll data (accounting records) > balance sheets, income statements etc (financial information)
❑ Inventory, work-in-progress, repair/maintenance and supply chain data (operations records) > production schedules, inventory systems, production monitoring systems
❑ Staff, appraisal, salary data (HR records) > employee performance and HR reports
❑ Marketing research, customer, purchase history data (marketing records) > marketing plans, sales reports etc
❑ Business intelligence, competitor, environmental data (strategic records) > industry trend reports, portfolio models, market share reports etc

>> *Support managers in implementing, controlling and evaluating strategies, plans, new products, new business models/ventures*

Decision support systems	Allow users to consider contingency planning ('what if?') scenarios > select best options
Strategic support systems	Allow users to measure/evaluate performance, analyse benchmarking data, receive exception reports
Enterprise resource planning	'Computer-based systems designed to process an organisation's transactions and facilitate integrated and real-time planning, production and customer response' *(CIPS)*. Cross-functional, enterprise-wide integration.

1.6 Analyse and explain how the use of information technology may help in the acquisition of P & S performance data

Supplier/vendor databases

A **database** is a centralised collection of structured data (usually computerised), which can be flexibly accessed by different users for different applications.

- ☑ Common data for all users to share: avoids duplication in individual user files
- ☑ Consistency in organisation's use of data: all work off same data, versions
- ☑ Continuity of knowledge: relationship/transaction data preserved over time
- ☑ Flexibility in how data can be interrogated, analysed, formatted for user needs
- ☑ Controlled access to amend/update data: avoids confusion, protects data integrity

SUPPLIER/VENDOR DATABASE

- Supplier details: contacts, products/materials available, prices, terms and conditions, quotations, plant and management etc
- Supplier appraisal and vendor rating reports, and approved/preferred supplier lists
- Current systems contracts, framework agreements and call-off contracts (buyers 'call off' orders as required, at terms agreed for the period)
- Vendor contract history and details
- Vendor performance history: quality, delivery, compliance etc.
- Prices charged for stock items by various suppliers
- Linked to databases for transactions (orders in progress, historical); inventory (stocks, usage rates, locations, value etc); market (availability, prices, trends).

- ❑ **Supplier selection**: 'best' suppliers (price, terms, performance) for purchases
- ❑ **Supplier performance** measurement and management
- ❑ **Contract management** (monitoring/controlling performance of contract terms)
- ❑ **Supplier base** development and rationalisation: identify valuable relationships, eliminate suppliers not required or duplicated
- ❑ **Supplier relationship management**: info > target, integrate, develop contacts

Stock movement and monitoring systems

- ☑ Capture point of sale, and stock delivery and movement information accurately (eg using barcode, RFID technology)
- ☑ Record stock movements and maintain stock balances
- ☑ Maintain stock integrity (identifying loss, damage, deterioration etc)
- ☑ Monitor productivity and utilisation > demand/capacity planning and measurement
- ☑ Automate stock control (re-order points, picking requirements etc)
- ☑ Evaluate (and model options) for stores layout and design, transport planning etc.
- ☑ Track and trace eg telematics, GPS > monitor logistics effectiveness/efficiency
- ☑ Flexible interrogation > management and statutory reports for performance management. *[KPIs for inventory management:* ***>> Unit 1.5]***

Analyse and explain how the use of information technology may help in the acquisition of P & S performance data 1.6

Electronic point of sale (EPOS) systems connect point-of-sale terminals to IT systems. POS data includes: product pricing, stock availability and location; product/line performance; and customer buying patterns.

Barcodes are code numbers printed as optical bars and read using a scanner: data is input direct to related database records. A more sophisticated technology is **Radio Frequency Identification (RFID)** which does not require scanning, so can be used for moving and less accessible items.

- ☑ Improved customer service information (eg on product availability, store location)
- ☑ Management information for sales analysis, demand forecasting and inventory control
- ☑ Efficient inventory management, via automatic stock replenishment

Quality monitoring and measurement systems

- ❑ Quality/service measures/KPIs: error rates, in-full-on-time deliveries etc
- ❑ Track record of supplier performance over time and against specification
- ❑ Sampling, observation or electronic monitoring/tracking data > statistics on defect rates, rejects/returns, customer complaints, production stoppages (in total, by material, by supplier)
- ❑ *Statistical process control (SPC)*: measurement of output samples during production > halt production to rectify faults outside defined tolerance limits for failure
- ❑ *Process capability analysis*: statistical measure of ability to reliably repeat performance eg number of defects per outputs, probabilities of process success or failure
- ❑ Evidence of supplier having management/control procedures in place to increase predictability and reliability of performance (eg via quality assurance)

Learning Objective 2.0: Measuring the performance of the supplier

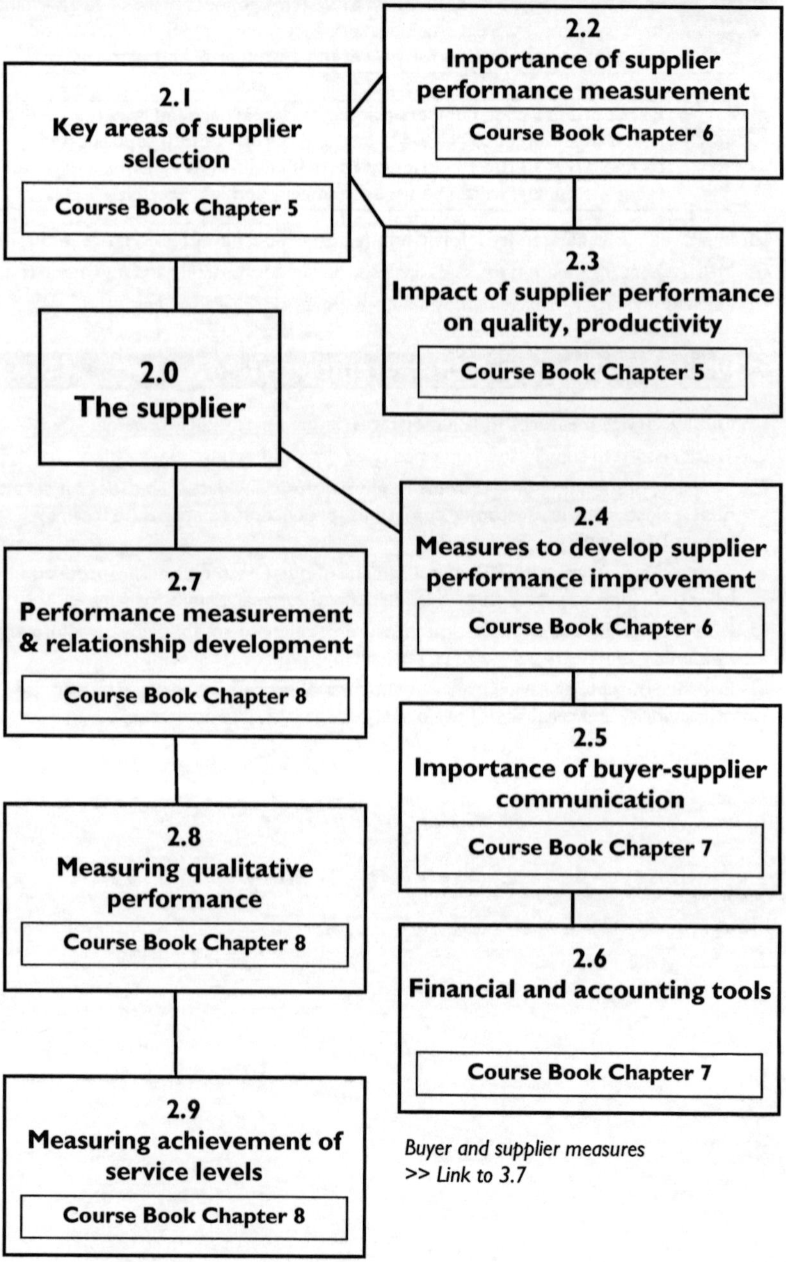

The buying process (purchasing cycle)

Recognition of a need
(eg requisition or bill of materials)

Authorised ↓

Definition/description of the need
(eg materials specification)

↓

Investigation & selection of potential suppliers

↓

Preparation and issue of purchase order

Authorised ↓

Follow-up of the order

↓

Processing of discrepancies and rejections
(late/incomplete delivery, faulty goods)

↓

Auditing of the transaction
(full conformance > pass for payment)

Authorised ↓

Closing the transaction
(reconcile order with goods received)

↓

Maintaining files and records

Considerations in making the purchasing decision

Supplier appraisal = performance assessment *prior to contract award* *[>> Unit 2.2]*

- ❑ *Low-value, non-critical items:* desk-based research into supplier quality/delivery performance (eg transaction history) or capability (eg customer references, samples)
- ❑ *More important items:* classify suppliers from which user departments can order without further checking:
  - **Approved supplier**: supplier satisfies certain basic technical and quality criteria
  - **Preferred supplier**: supplier has a track record of satisfactory performance
- ❑ *Critical items:* more rigorous measurement required before contract award: eg site visits, external supplier accreditation (eg ISO 9000 quality assurance).

Basic variables in purchasing decisions

- Price and value for money (esp. competitive tendering eg in public sector)
- Relationship with supplier (dependability, loyalty, flexibility, goodwill, compatibility, willingness to partner, willingness to pursue continuous improvement)
- Specific requirements (eg reverse logistics/storage capability, local supply)
- Quality, conformance to specification (and process capability: reliability of quality performance)
- Availability/delivery (and reliability of delivery performance: on-time, in-full supply)
- Compliance (with legal, environmental and ethical standards and policies)

2.2 Explain the importance of measuring a supplier's performance and distinguish [this] from supplier appraisal

Supplier assessment

Supplier appraisal	→	Vendor rating
Pre-contract evaluation of a potential supplier's **capability** to fulfil buyer requirements: ability reliably to control quality/price/ quantity delivery.	*Supplier selection (contract award)*	Evaluation of a current supplier's **performance** in fulfilling contract/service requirements: comparison v standards, previous orders, other suppliers etc.

Supplier development

Feedback, finance or assistance offered to a supplier (pre- or post-contract) to support the supplier in fulfilling buyer requirements (for products/services or interface).

Supplier appraisal

When needed?

- ❑ To manage supply risk: ongoing control of sources of strategic/critical items
- ❑ Identify/qualify new sources for strategic/critical items
- ❑ Identify/select sources of new or one-off products/services

Four-stage process for supplier appraisal *(CIPS)*

Stage	
Plan and prepare ↓	Check internal policies, criteria and existing data on suppliers; decide assessment scope
Supplier assessments ↓	Various methods of supplier appraisal: eg 10 Cs, FACE2FACE
Evaluate and report results ↓	Evaluate appraisal data in light of criteria
Recommendation and feedback	Recommend supplier + feed back results to suppliers (> relationship-building, info for improvement, non-judgemental focus)

Supply market information (purchasing research)

[>> Unit 1.3]

Supplier information

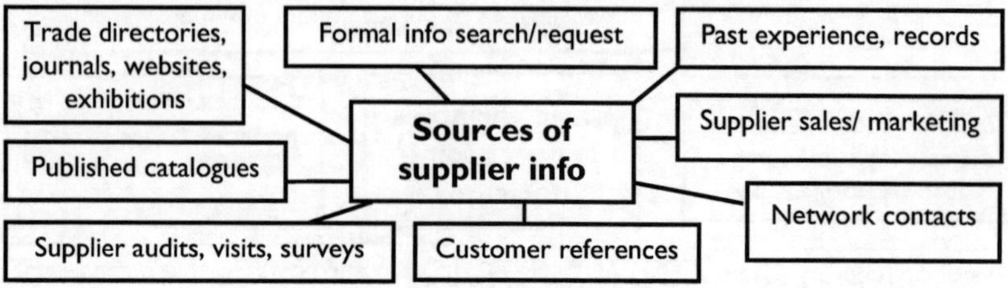

Criteria for assessing supplier desirability/capability

Lysons & Farrington	*Ten Cs* **[>> Unit 2.4]**	*Baily, Farmer & Jessop*
Adequacy and care of production equipment Personal attitudes Means of controlling quality Housekeeping Competence: technical staff Competence: management	Competence Capacity Costs Commitment (to quality) Control (of processes) Cash (financial stability) Consistency (of output) Cultural compatibility Clean (environmentally) Compliance (or CSR)	Task variables eg quality, service and price Financial stability Good management Results of site visits Ability to support EDI JIT capabilities

FACE 2 FACE

Fixed assets *Physical resources to meet buyer needs* • Check age of main fixed assets (Due for replacement? Finance available?)	**Financial stability** *Continuity of supply; ability to maintain quality, meet financial claims etc* • Check published accounts re gearing, profitability, liquidity
Ability to deliver the goods *Reliability of delivery/quality/service* • Get references from existing customers • Check process/output samples	**Ability to work with buyer** *Compatibility of culture* • Assess relationship via negotiation and on-site visits
Cost *Competitive total acquisition costs* • Price comparisons • Price/cost analysis • Willingness to negotiate terms	**Commitment to quality** • Check control systems, certification • Check process capability (eg via SPC) • Check process/output samples • Ability/willingness to improve
Efficiency • Check speed of stock turnover, speed of collecting debtor balances etc	**Environmental factors** • Check policy statements, certification, reverse logistics/recycling capability etc

Supplier auditing (on-site visits or capability surveys)

☑ Important source of info (by questionnaire, observation and on-site interviews) on:

- Production equipment, operations and capacity
- Operation of key materials management activities
- Expertise and motivation of personnel
- Technological know-how of supervisors and management capabilities

☒ Costly, time-consuming approach: reserve for strategic items, short-listed suppliers

2.2 Explain the importance of measuring a supplier's performance and distinguish [this] from supplier appraisal

The supplier's perspective on supplier appraisal

Reason for supplier reluctance	*Steps a buyer can take*
Bad experiences of previous appraisals, possibly with other buyers	Conduct process fairly and transparently
Unsure of supplier selection process (or suspicious eg of other supplier 'inside track', being used as benchmark)	Provide full information about the process; keep suppliers informed about progress; give constructive feedback
Timing may be inconvenient	Give preparation time; avoid busy periods
Belief that the process will be expensive and time-consuming	Streamline the exercise as far as possible, consistent with obtaining info required
Reluctance to share confidential info	Be prepared to sign confidentiality agreement

NB: objective is to position organisation as **attractive potential customer** > successful *and* unsuccessful (possible future) suppliers.

- Positive impression created of buyers and organisation > potential for future business
- Process is seen to be handled fairly and efficiently
- Constructive feedback offered to support supplier improvements and added value

The **supplier preferencing** model appraises supply relationships from the supplier's point of view, according to the desirability of buyers.

Buyer attractiveness factors:

eg

Glamour or high profile
Reputation (eg CSR)
Fair dealing, prompt payment
Info-sharing, collaboration
Financial viability, success
Future plans

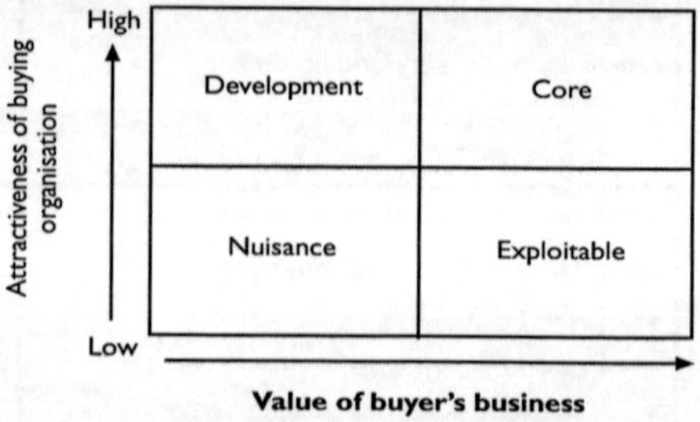

Quadrant	*Supplier priority*
Nuisance	Terminate non-viable customers – or raise prices > worthwhile.
Exploitable	Maximise potential profit from large business volume. Comply with terms of contract but no more: charge for any 'extras'.
Development	Secure relationship for potential future growth in business. 'Go the extra mile' >> move customer to Core status.
Core customers	Maintain close long-term relationship. Regular contact > monitor threats/opportunities; offer added value.

NB: transactional/competitive relationships, buyer has no need to be 'attractive', but for strategic supplies > attention to developing/maintaining 'good customer' status.

Explain the importance of measuring a supplier's performance and distinguish [this] from supplier appraisal 2.2

Supplier performance measurement

Supplier performance measurement = comparison of current supplier (vendor) performance against:

- Defined performance criteria or key performance indicators
- Previous performance (to identify deterioration/improvement trends)
- Other supplier's performance or standard benchmarks (to maintain competitive supplier selection and incentive for vendor improvement)

Why important?

- ❑ To show seriousness of performance criteria and expectations: motivate performance and improvement, support culture of excellence (own and supplier)
- ❑ To manage supply risk: ongoing control of quality, delivery, value for money, continuity of supply (especially important with strategic/critical items)
- ❑ To support and enhance the organisation's quality and productivity *[>> Unit 2.3]*
- ❑ To support contract management: ensuring that agreed benefits are obtained
- ❑ To identify approved/preferred suppliers to support efficient user-department buying
- ❑ To identify suppliers with potential for closer partnership, co-makership or strategic alliance
- ❑ To provide feedback for learning and continuous improvement of performance (own and supplier)
- ❑ To provide benchmark standards for future supplier appraisal and vendor rating
- ❑ To evaluate the effectiveness of the supplier appraisal/selection process: ability to predict subsequent performance, effect on supplier relationships
- ❑ To supply management information for planning, control, supply chain strategy etc

Key performance indicators (KPIs) for suppliers

Success factors	Sample KPIs
Price	Basic purchase price Profit margin earned by supplier Price compared with other suppliers
Quality	Reject rates for manufactured items Adherence to quality standards (eg ISO 9000) Frequency of service failure in service contracts
Delivery	Frequency of late delivery Frequency of incorrect or incomplete delivery
Service	Promptness in dealing with enquiries and problems Adherence to agreements on after-sales service
Financial stability	Ability to meet financial commitments and claims Ability to maintain quality and delivery
Overall performance	Benchmarking against other suppliers

2.2 Explain the importance of measuring a supplier's performance and distinguish [this] from supplier appraisal

Performance measurement tools (CIPS)

Systems and information tools	• Systems eg materials requirements planning (MRP), enterprise resource planning (ERP), performance monitoring software. • Info from suppliers, vendor database, buyer knowledge
Performance measurement and accreditation tools	• Vendor rating ***[>> Unit 2.4]*** • Financial ratios ***[>> Unit 2.4]*** • Carter's 10 Cs ***[>> Unit 2.4]*** • National/international standards and benchmarks eg ISO 9000 ***[>> Unit 2.8]***
General management tools *(NB: also applied to P & S function)*	• SWOT analysis: strengths/weaknesses of suppliers in relation to environmental opportunities/threats ***[>> Unit 2.4*** • Tools for prioritising supplies (eg Pareto analysis) and type of supply relationships/KPIs best suited (eg *Kraljic matrix*)

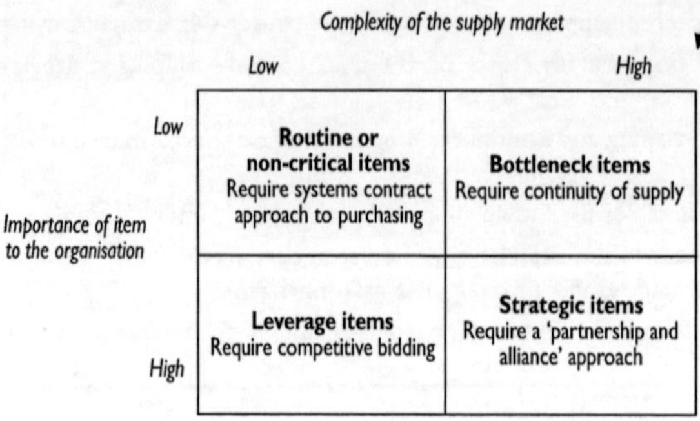

- *Non-critical:* KPI = functional efficiency
- *Leverage:* KPI = cost/price and materials flow management
- *Bottleneck:* KPI = cost management and reliable short-term sourcing
- *Strategic:* KPI = long term supply continuity

NB: Methods may be:
- **Numerical/statistical** – eg vendor rating, financial ratios
- **Perception based** – eg Carter's 10Cs, stakeholder feedback
- **Research based** – eg financial accounts, credit references, customer references
- **Accreditation based** (comparison with published standards) – eg ISO 9000
- **Self-assessment based** – eg supplier reports, audits

Third party tools for supplier performance measurement

- ❑ Market research specialists > identify possible suppliers within a market
- ❑ Financial specialists > assess financial stability of supplier (including statutory audit)
- ❑ Consultants > vet supplier for compliance with quality standards/benchmarks
- ❑ Technical specialists > monitor supplier performance eg on construction, IT projects
- ❑ Consultants > devise, implement, maintain or audit organisation's performance measurement systems (eg process audit, value for money audit)

'Good' supplier performance

- ☐ Allows the buying organisation to perform **efficiently** and **effectively**
- ☐ Enhanced **productivity** at lower **costs of operation**:
  - ☑ Reliability/continuity of supply > avoid costs of stockouts, stopped production
  - ☑ Flexibility/speed of supply supports just in time supply (minimising inventory costs) and 'lean' production (reducing costs and maximising value by removing waste from all processes)
  - ☑ Flexibility/speed of supply supports 'agility': ability to respond to changing market/customer needs > product modification, shorter product lifecycles
  - ☑ Approved supplier status supports efficient user-department buying and focused use of P & S function
  - ☑ Preferred or single supplier status > potential for call-off contracts, lower supplier selection/contracting/transaction costs
  - ☑ Potential to integrate systems > streamlined demand/capacity planning, processes
  - ☑ Potential to partner/collaborate longer-term on value analysis/engineering, efficiency gains, cost savings
  - ☑ Quality/delivery > maintain value at lower price (value for money)
- ☐ Enhanced **quality** at lower cost:
  - ☑ Quality inputs > quality outputs: applies across whole 'quality chain' from suppliers to ultimate consumer
  - ☑ Costs of prevention *lower* than costs of failure > quality assurance/improvement lowers costs of quality
  - ☑ 'Get it right first time, every time' (zero defects) approach > emphasis on defect *prevention* rather than defect *detection:* lower inspection costs, reject/scrap/rework costs, customer complaint costs, reputational damage costs etc
  - ☑ Expert contribution to new product design, specification > enhanced quality
  - ☑ Flexibility/speed of supply and quality of information supports customer service: speed of response to customer queries/requests, delivery expectations
  - ☑ Value added to products eg by recommendation/supply of high-quality components, self-inspection of work in progress
  - ☑ Willingness to collaborate on quality problem-solving, seek continuous improvement, joint staff training and development etc.

'Poor' supplier performance

- ☒ Poor quality inputs > poor quality outputs
- ☒ Quality/delivery failure > added costs of disruption to production, inspection, rejects, re-working, complaint adjustment etc + managerial time
- ☒ Knock-on effects of supplier failure > loss of customer goodwill, reputational damage, poor employee morale, conflict, poor perception of P & S
- ☒ Unreliability of delivery > need for excess safety/buffer stocks > increased costs of stock holding, risk of obsolescence/damage/deterioration etc
- ☒ Inability to develop lean, agile supply chain strategies, based on collaborative, trusting supply relationships
- ☒ Unacceptable exposure to supply risk > added costs of risk mitigation: insurances, multiple suppliers (> loss of supply efficiency) etc.

Stakeholders in supplier performance

Stakeholder group	Interest in supplier performance	Contribution to measurement system
Purchasing and supply function	Support for own performance (achievement of Five Rights); support for credibility/status in organisation; potential to develop effective supply chain strategies	Overall responsibility; leadership and management; coordination and implementation; review and feedback
Suppliers	Own competitive advantage, reputation, survival/growth, retained goodwill/custom of buyer, potential for sharing value gains	Provision of measurement data; ideas for improvement; feedback on buyer's performance; in some cases, self-assessment
User departments	Fulfilment of operational requirements; life-time costs of meeting requirements; potential for added value, synergy, innovation	Input re criteria and requirements of system; technical expertise; feedback on supplier performance
Other internal departments	Fulfilment of requirements in area of expertise (eg budgetary conformance, innovation)	Financial appraisal; staffing issues; assessment of supplier's production and R&D
External third parties	Ethical trading, employment and environmental practices; consumer safety and rights; security and accessible pricing of supply (eg for essential services); statutory reports and returns; sustainable business survival/growth etc.	Influence on KPIs used (eg public sector compulsory competitive tendering, CSR/ethical codes/guidelines); input to design, implementation and assessment of the performance management system itself ***[>> Unit 2.2]***

Analyse and explain measures to develop sustained improvement of supplier performance 2.4

10 Cs model of performance measures (*Carter*)

Competence of all staff (managers, sales/technical/production etc)
Capacity to fulfil requirements (sufficient production/financial capacity etc)
Cost (competitive total acquisition cost – including service, maintenance, repair etc)
Commitment to quality (evidenced by quality systems, external accreditation etc)
Control of processes (ie process capability > reliably repeat performance)
Cash (financial stability and potential for investment in improvement)
Consistency of output, delivery and service
Cultural compatibility (ability to work with buyer; potential integration/synergy)
Cleanliness (sustainable resource use, pollution/waste control, recycling/disposal etc)
Compliance (or corporate social responsibility: ethical trading/employment practices)

Vendor rating

☑ Quantitative measures of price, quality and delivery aspects of supplier performance:
- **Price**: price history, comparison with competitors
- **Quality**: % rejects, number of production line hold-ups etc
- **Delivery**: number/% deliveries on-time-in-full, one day late etc.

☒ Requires extensive data collection/processing: only worthwhile for strategic items.
☒ Does not address causes of problems (eg supplier- or buyer-side inefficiency)
☒ Evaluation, weightings etc subjective (> supplement with supplier audits)

Planning ↓	Agreed use of vendor rating at contract Planned approach, criteria, weightings etc
Introduction ↓	System may need to be piloted to test methods/reporting mechanisms
Action, monitoring, feedback ↓	Buyer investigates results and feeds back > supplier improvement planning
Re-engineering ↓	Supplier implements agreed process changes
Action, monitoring, feedback ↓	Monitoring, feedback, adjustment forms an ongoing cycle, until relationship ends.
Closedown	Scheme terminated and reviewed > learning and improvement of process

Checklist method ***(Full example: see Chapter 6 of Course Book)***

Performance factors	**Good**	**Satisfactory**	**Unsatisfactory**
Purchasing			
Delivers on schedule	☐	☐	☐
Delivers at quoted price	☐	☐	☐
Prices are competitive	☐	☐	☐

Factor rating method

Performance factor	Weighting	Score	Rating
Price	0.4	0.94	0.376
Quality	0.4	0.97	0.388
Delivery	0.2	0.72	0.144
Overall evaluation	1.0		0.908

Use of financial ratios

Ratio analysis is used to calculate performance indicators which can be compared with: performance in previous years (to highlight trends); budgeted (v actual) performance in the current year; and/or the performance of other suppliers businesses (to highlight strengths and weaknesses).

Eg: *profitability* ratios (extent to which firm has traded profitably); *liquidity* ratios (extent to which firm has liquid assets to meet short/long-term liabilities); *efficiency* ratios (efficiency with which firm is managing its assets). *[>> Unit 2.6]*

Supplier SWOT analysis

Strengths *(internal, positive)* Advantages compared to competitors? Access to unique (or lower cost) resources? Strengths as perceived by market (including existing customers)?	**Weaknesses** *(internal, limiting)* Aspects of performance to be improved? Managerial, operational, technological or financial limitations constraining activities? Weaknesses as perceived by market (including existing customers)?
Opportunities *(external, exploitable)* Potential contracts/relationships? Changes in technology that are (or could be) exploited to improve performance? Favourable market trends that could be exploited to benefit?	**Threats** *(external, limiting/threatening)* How well placed to respond to competitive pressures? Technological developments? Regulation changes? Resource scarcity? Any significant problems with cashflow (including likely bad debts)?

Cycle of performance review meetings

- ❑ Daily/weekly: routine (e-mail/automated) buyer/supplier contact > note problems
- ❑ Monthly: meeting for review of problems and progress > pass on recommendations
- ❑ Quarterly: meeting for review of problems and progress > pass on recommendations
- ❑ Annually: senior stakeholders meet to formally review/ratify plans
- ❑ Ad hoc: response to emergencies (involving appropriate decision makers)

Evaluate the importance of close and frequent buyer-supplier communication 2.5

Demand/supply chain relationships

The **supply chain** 'encompasses all organisations and activities associated with the flow and transformation of goods from the raw materials stage, through to the end user, as well as the associated information flows.' *(Handfield & Nichols)*

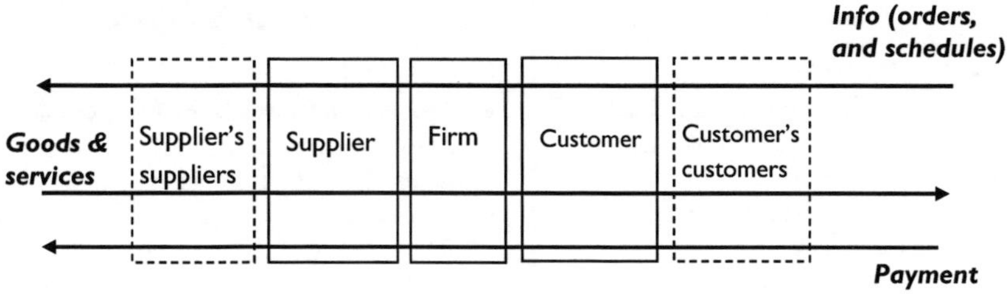

- ❑ **Supply chain** = creation of supply, or fulfilment > 'push' from supplier end
- ❑ **Demand chain** = creation of demand by market > 'pull' from customer end
  'Demand chain management would be a better term, and would stress the fact that the chain is driven by market forces and not by the supply side' *(Christopher)*.

The relationship spectrum

The **relationship spectrum** illustrates the range of relationships at various degrees of closeness or collaboration.

Competitive ⟷ Collaborative

Relationship type	*Characteristics*
Adversarial relationship	Buyer and supplier are 'opponents', striving to obtain commercial advantage at the other's expense. Little trust, communication or cooperation: potential for conflict.
Transactional relationship	May reflect more frequent requirement on the part of the buyer, but still low-collaboration purchase of low-value, low-risk supplies.
Strategic alliance	Two (or more) organisations develop contractual collaboration to deliver a joint offering for mutual benefit. Eg a software developer allies with IT trainer to offer added value software + training package.
Partnership relationship	Buyer and supplier agree to collaborate closely for the long term, sharing information and ideas for development. Very high level of trust: aim is to find solutions that benefit both parties without detriment to either.

2.5 Evaluate the importance of close and frequent buyer-supplier communication

Competitive v collaborative relationships

Competitive	Collaborative
Buying organisation seeks to obtain the best price possible, at the expense of the supplier's profit margin (and *vice versa*).	Buying organisation seeks to develop long-term relationship with supplier: work together to add value, to mutual benefit.
No recognition of mutual interests: simple exchanges between buyer/seller.	Proactive joint search for improvements and innovations > share in benefits.
Adversarial style: • Distant (formal) communications • Win-lose approach to negotiations • Lack of trust • Little direct contact or info sharing • Emphasis on single transactions, short-term contracts, tight controls	Not 'cosy' relationship: • Joint search for efficiency, improvement • Agreed dovetailed objectives • Openness and transparency • Relationship of equal partners • Recognise need for exit strategy: no complacency

Benefits of competition:	Benefits of collaboration:
☑ Obtains value for buyer that would otherwise be retained by supplier (as profit margin) ☑ Minimises costs of relationship development and management where unnecessary	☑ Established points of contact > trust ☑ Awareness of capabilities/requirements > managed expectations, better service ☑ Sharing data/plans > forward planning, joint product/service development, joint performance measurement ☑ Pooled expertise > quality, added value ☑ Reduced transaction costs (and potential for further cost reductions)

- *80:20 rule (Pareto principle):* invest in collaborative relationships with small number of important suppliers/items (eg using supply positioning models)
- *Adversarial-collaborative relationships:* buyer works collaboratively with supplier at operational level to increase value – but competes commercially to appropriate as much of value as possible (eg in price negotiation)

Close and frequent buyer-supplier communications

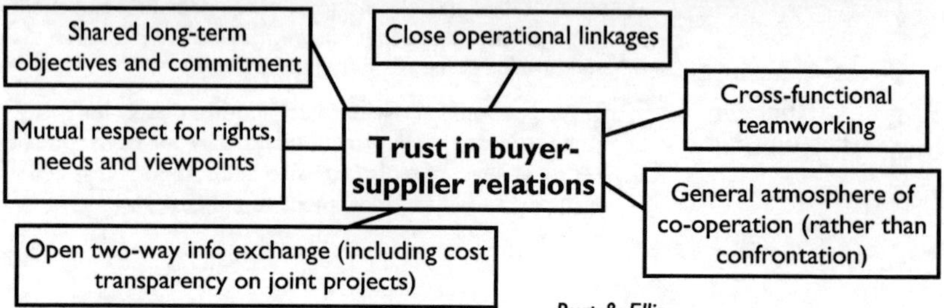

Burt & Ellis

Evaluate the importance of close and frequent buyer-supplier communication 2.5

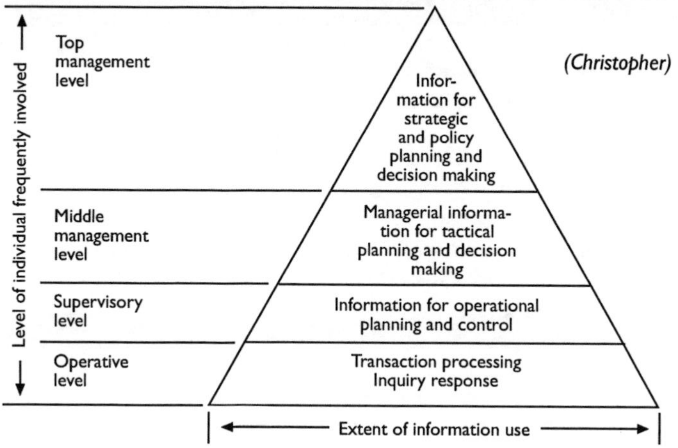

Resolving conflict and disputes

Thomas-Kilmann model:

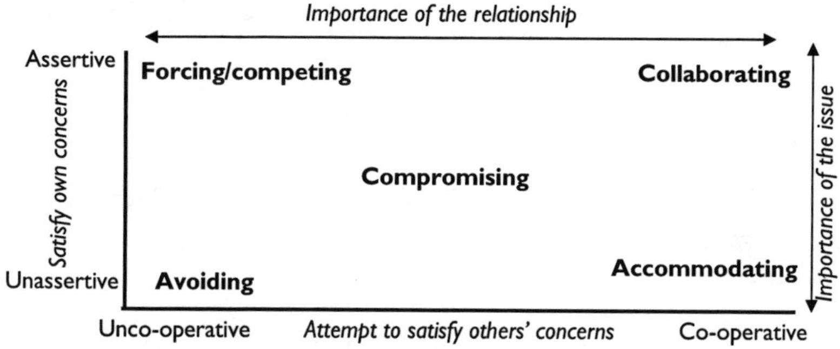

- *Avoiding:* you withdraw from conflict or attempt to sweep under the carpet
- *Forcing/competing:* you impose your solution on the problem
- *Accommodating:* you concede the issue without a fight, to preserve harmony
- *Compromising:* you bargain/negotiate, so each party trades concessions for gains
- *Collaborating:* both parties work to find a 'win-win' to clearly stated needs

Dispute resolution mechanisms in buyer-supplier relations:

- ❑ Informal conflict resolution
- ❑ Internal escalation: dispute passed to a higher level of management for resolution
- ❑ Mediation: third party hears opposing cases and facilitates process > agreement
- ❑ Arbitration: third party hears opposing cases and makes a binding judgement
- ❑ Re-negotiation: parties decide to re-negotiate contract terms > new agreement
- ❑ Litigation: one or other party initiates legal action before the courts

Benefits of shared measurement approaches

- Joint buyer/supplier performance measures > focus on mutual benefits and value gains > support collaboration and partnership
- Motivates both parties to seek improvement and integrates improvements > process alignment
- Mutual understanding of each others' aims, constraints > potential for joint problem-solving, innovation for improvement
- Ethical, relationship-building approach: minimises dominance/exploitation issues
- Supports supply chain perspective: weighs overall efficiency and competitive power of total supply chain (not just individual organisations)

Financial/accounting tools

NB: this is a brief overview: see detailed coverage in Chapter 7 of your Course Book.

Cashflow analysis

Cashflow statement:

- Sources of cash coming into business (eg cash surplus from operating activities, new share capital)
- Cash outgoings/spending (interest payments, loan repayments, taxation, expenditure on assets, dividends to shareholders)
- Overall cash surplus or deficit at beginning of year, during year, at end of year (> comparison to identify improving/worsening position)

Profitability ratios

Ratio	***Calculation***	***Uses***
Gross profit percentage (profit margin)	Gross profit as % of turnover $\frac{\text{Gross profit}}{\text{Sales}} \times 100$	Calculate for different years to show profit margin increase or decrease. (Doesn't account for sales mix changes etc.)
Net profit percentage	Net profit as % of turnover. $\frac{\text{Profit before tax}}{\text{Sales}} \times 100$	Eg an increase would indicate increased selling prices, reduced input costs or more efficiently controlled overheads
Return on capital employed (ROCE) *[Primary ratio]*	Operating profit (before interest and tax) as % of capital employed (long-term capital invested in the business). $\frac{\text{Operating profit}}{\text{Average capital employed}} \times 100$	Return company makes on amounts invested in it by shareholders and suppliers of debt capital. To improve: increase profit margin on sales *or* increase rate of asset turnover [see below]

Employ appropriate financial and accounting tools to assess organisational efficiency 2.6

Short-term liquidity ratios

***Liquidity** is the availability of current assets ('ready' assets, like stock, debtors and cash) to meet current liabilities (amounts owing in the near future).*

Ratio	*Calculation*	*Uses*
Current (working capital) ratio	Liquid assets (eg cash, debtors, saleable stocks) in relation to current liabilities. $\frac{\text{Current assets}}{\text{Current liabilities}}$	Indicates (in)sufficient current assets to cover current liabilities. Show changes in liquidity year on year, or compare with other firms. ('Ideal' = 2.)
Quick (acid test *or* liquidity) ratio	Liquid assets *(excluding stock)* as % of current liabilities. $\frac{\text{Current assets} - \text{stock}}{\text{Current liabilities}}$	Focus on most liquid assets (cash, debtors): can *quickly* be used to pay debts. If ratio low, those payable in near future may not be fully covered. ('Ideal' = 1.)

Efficiency ratios *(measuring the efficiency with which a firm is managing its assets)*

Ratio	*Calculation*	*Uses*
Asset turnover	Number of times per year average operating assets are 'turned over' (sold). $\frac{\text{Sales}}{\text{Operating assets}}$ = times/year	Indicates how well assets are being used to generate sales: eg ratio of 1.4 means that for every £1 of assets employed, £1.40 sales revenue generated. Ratio should be high as possible!

NB **ROCE** can be expressed as: (Profitability x asset turnover ratios) $\frac{\textbf{Operating profit}}{\textbf{Sales}} \times \frac{\textbf{Sales}}{\textbf{Operating assets}}$

To improve ROCE: increase profit margin on sales OR increase rate of asset turnover

Identification of supplier fraud

Possible indicators of fraud, corruption or conflicts of interest in suppliers:

- ❑ Insistence on payment in cash (avoidance of records > cover theft, tax evasion etc?)
- ❑ Unusual patterns in dealing with tenders eg repeated success (possibility of collusion)
- ❑ Evidence of close relationship between buyer/seller eg gifts/hospitality, personal or business relationship (possibility of inducement/influence on buying decisions)

Fraud prevention measures:

- ❑ Ethical codes > recruitment, selection, appraisal, development of purchasing staff
- ❑ Strong standards of corporate governance and ethics from top management down
- ❑ Communication of ethical standards to suppliers
- ❑ Rotating of buyer responsibilities to avoid collusion, conflicts of interest
- ❑ Division of responsibilities: eg contract awarder/orderer not also payment authoriser
- ❑ Checks and reconciliations: eg orders v receipts v invoices; reviews of patterns of spending on purchasing cards etc.

2.7 Analyse the use of performance measurement as a tool for supplier relationship development

Relationship development

Buyer's perspective	*Supplier's perspective*
☑ Familiarity: less risk of disputes, misunderstood requirements etc ☑ Less cost of supplier identification, tendering etc ☑ Quality/delivery problems ironed out over time, with collaboration ☑ Goodwill > flexibility in emergency ☑ Motivation for suppliers to invest in R & D > lower-cost solutions etc	☑ Familiarity: less risk of disputes, misunderstood requirements, rejects ☑ Less need for/cost of direct selling ☑ Managerial time freed for focus on cost savings, added value, business development ☑ Trust in payment, future business > better revenue/cashflow and capacity planning

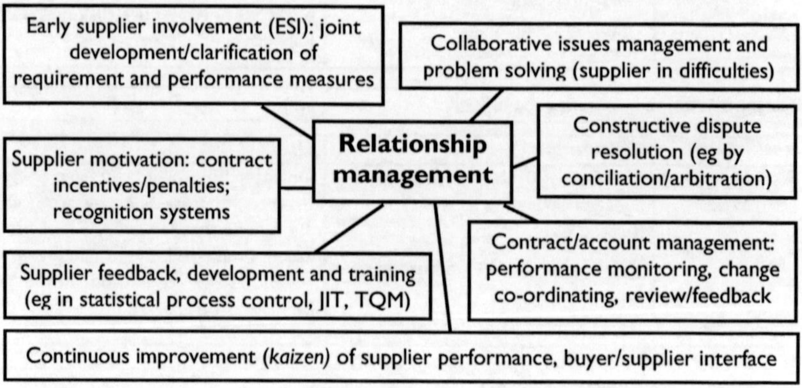

Performance measurement as a tool of relationship development

- ❑ Measurement **encourages communication** re requirements, expectations, constraints etc > better planning info, increasing trust, mutual understanding
- ❑ **Joint development** of performance measures (eg in ESI) > ensures mutual benefit, less risk of misunderstanding/disappointment > enhanced trust, commitment
- ❑ Measurement key to **development and training** processes: systematic performance-relevant feedback for training needs identification
- ❑ Measurement key to **continuous improvement**: ongoing info for identification of weaknesses, problems, needs/opportunities for improvement planning
- ❑ Measurement key to **contract/account management**: evidence of failure in meeting contract terms; objective focus for problem-solving; source of feedback to suppliers; evidence in event of dispute
- ❑ Measurement = **motivating factor for both parties**: benchmarks for buyer and supplier performance and interface/relationship between them
- ❑ Approach to measurement **sets tone of relationship.** Coercive/manipulative approach may undermine collaboration, reduce buyer's attractiveness as a customer. Shared measures, joint problem-solving, value-sharing, feedback, info-sharing > trust

Analyse the use of performance measurement as a tool for supplier relationship development 2.7

Supplier development

Supplier development is the process whereby a buying organisation assists a supplier to fulfil its requirements.

Approaches to supplier development:

- ❑ Enhancing working relationships (eg by improved communication systems, routines)
- ❑ Increasing performance goals and requiring supplier capability improvements
- ❑ Providing support personnel and best-practice training
- ❑ Providing capital or equipment to support improvements (eg buyer pays for terminals to support buyer use of purchasing cards)
- ❑ Sharing value gains (added sales, savings) and risks/costs of development projects

Buyer's perspective	***Supplier's perspective***
☑ Support for outsourcing strategy ☑ Improving time-to-market, new product development, quality, delivery > increased profitability ☑ Streamlining systems for process efficiencies, cost savings ☑ Gaining discounts or other benefits as a *quid pro quo* for development	☑ Production and process efficiencies, cost savings > profitability ☑ Improvement in customer satisfaction > retained/increased business ☑ Improved capacity, service levels > additional sales to other customers ☑ Direct gains in knowledge, resources, ☑ Enhanced learning, flexibility
☒ Managerial costs in identifying and negotiating opportunities ☒ Cost of activities and resources: risk of over-investment ☒ Risk of sharing intellectual property	☒ Managerial costs ☒ Investment in systems/infra-structure ☒ Cost of discounts or exclusivity agreements given as *quid pro quo* ☒ Risks of over-dependence

Performance measurement as a tool of supplier development

- ❑ Tools eg Pareto analysis, Kraljic matrix used to **prioritise supplies** > focus development resources on key suppliers
- ❑ Measurement used to **identify needs/opportunities** requiring improvement/development of key suppliers
- ❑ Definition, monitoring and evaluation of key performance metrics > **planning and control** of supplier development projects
- ❑ Measurement = **motivating factor for suppliers**: need to meet improvement goals to earn benefits given
- ❑ Measurement = **motivating factor for buyers**: need to secure improvement goals from supplier to justify expense/effort of development

2.8 Analyse qualitative supplier performance measures

Qualitative aspects of supplier performance

Quantitative measures	Qualitative measures
Easier to define KPIs, monitor over time	KPIs, monitoring likely to be subjective
Focus on efficiency	Focus on effectiveness
Suit purchase of products (tangibles)	Suit purchase of services (intangibles)
Eg price, total cost of ownership, on-time-in-full deliveries, error/defect rates	Eg

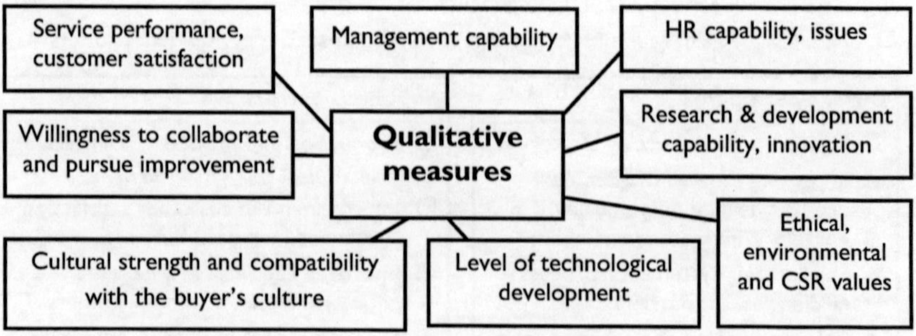

Measured according to:

- ❑ Specific agreed standards (as defined in contract, service level agreement etc)
- ❑ Established industry norms
- ❑ Buyer's past performance (yardstick to measure improvement/deterioration)
- ❑ Performance of other suppliers (including internal and former suppliers of the same product or service)
- ❑ Accreditation under national and international standards/benchmarks

Eg *measures of R & D capability*
Financial investment in R & D
Number of R & D staff employed
Quality and extent of R & D facilities
Past record in R & D innovation
Stated R & D/innovation objectives
Willingness to share ideas, innovative solutions > early involvement
External R & D contacts/outsourcing

Eg *measures of cultural adaptation*
Cultural strength: values powerful, shared
Cultural health: values positive, adaptive
Compatibility of culture with buyer culture
Skills, values and style of management
Commitment to staff development
Mission/vision/strategy of organisation: fit with buyer plans
CSR/ethical policies (through supply chain)

Benchmarking

Benchmarking is 'a continuous process of measuring products, services and practices against those of competitors or industry leaders, in order to plan improvements against those standards'.

Type	*Focus*
Competitive	Comparing the organisation's performance with industry competitors. (Accessibility, reliability and comparability of data can be a problem...)
Functional/ generic	Comparing specific functions (eg R & D) across industries > continuous improvement and demonstrable competitive edge.

- ☑ Learning from the successes (and mistakes) of others > confidence, flexibility
- ☑ Build supply chain competitive advantage by matching competitor performance
- ☑ Enhances supplier motivation through competitive element
- ☑ Heightened awareness of performance measures > improvement planning
- ☑ Increased improvement-focused communication and collaboration

- ☒ Complex, time-consuming and costly to implement properly
- ☒ May create pressure for change – without commitment or resources to back it up
- ☒ Depends on availability of accurate, up-to-date, transparent information
- ☒ May stifle supplier creativity, innovation (preference for 'copying')

Ethical issues: how competitor information is provided or obtained; unrealistic standards imposed on less developed suppliers (may adversely affect business sustainability, worker conditions)...

National and international standards

- Many countries have organisations that establish and monitor technical/safety standards > ensure specifications meet accepted criteria. Eg BSI (UK)
- European standards committees eg CEN > standards institute publishing European technical standards (EN). Adopted international standard ISO 9000 > European standard EN 29000.
- International Organisation for Standardisation (ISO): publishes technical agreements re tolerances, technical drawings, recognised symbols etc > global standards.

ISO 9000 quality standards

- ❑ ISO 9001: 2000 (requirements for quality management systems)
- ❑ ISO 9000: 2000 and ISO 9004: 2000 (voluntary guidelines)

Quality principles of ISO 9000:

1. Focus on your customers
2. Provide leadership
3. Involve your people
4. Use a process approach
5. Take a systems approach
6. Encourage continual improvement
7. Get the facts before you decide
8. Work with your suppliers

Measuring service performance

A **service** is 'any activity of benefit that one party can offer to another that is essentially intangible and does not result in the ownership of anything. Its production may or may not be tied to a physical product.' *(Kotler)*

Intangibility	Services have no tactile/visual presence to indicate value/attributes.
Inseparability	Services are produced and consumed at the same time.
Heterogeneity	Service elements/quality cannot be standardised.
Perishability	Services cannot be stored: provision must meet fluctuating demand.
Ownership	Services do not result in transfer of ownership of anything.

↓ *From a purchaser's point of view*

Key characteristics *(Baily et al)*
• Impracticability of storage
• Lack of inspectability
• Uncertainty in contractual agreements
• Complexity: mix of product (materials, accessories) and service elements

Performance measurement issues
• Fluctuating demands on delivery
• Difficult to specify/measure compliance
• Difficult to assign responsibilities/costs
• People + Process (+ Product/Price) factors

>> Particular need for purchasing involvement and discipline.

- ❑ *Pre-contract detail:* agreeing service levels, schedules and basis for charges
- ❑ *Service specification:* involving purchasing expertise *plus* user groups
- ❑ *Service level agreement:* [see below]
- ❑ *Supplier management:* reinforcing expectations, standards
- ❑ *Quality assurance:* supplier selection/appraisal; supplier relationship management

Service specification

Quality elements in specifying services *(Parasuraman)*
Reliability (how consistently and dependably supplier provides the service)
Access (how easy it is to contact supplier)
Competence (skill and knowledge with which supplier staff supply service)
Credibility (supplier trustworthiness)
Understanding (supplier attempt to understand customer requirements)
Responsiveness (prompt/willing service)
Tangibles (physical goods as part of service)
Courtesy (of supplier staff)
Communication (how often/understandably supplier keeps customer informed)
Security (management of customer risk)

Service level agreements

- ❑ How often is the service to be provided?
- ❑ During what hours will the service be carried out?
- ❑ How many staff (and, if relevant, what grades of staff at what pay rates) will be involved? (> impact on quality)
- ❑ How far (ie to what specific tasks) will the service extend (and not extend)?
- ❑ Does the service include special tasks caused by fault of the customer's staff?
- ❑ What qualifications are needed by the staff members providing the service?
- ❑ What speed of response is expected when the customer makes a request?
- ❑ What procedures will be used to resolve disputes?

Measures of supplier achievement of agreed service levels

Customer satisfaction	Feedback (formal/informal) on service v expectations Complaints, claims, returns for reasons of poor quality
Order fulfilment	Eg number of orders completely satisfied over period; percentage volume/value of each order completed accurately (correct items/quantities)
Delivery lead time	Eg percentage of orders delivered on time; average lead times; 'emergency' orders fulfilled on time
Process efficiency	Activities carried out to budgeted cost/schedule or specified criteria (eg response times) Cost of initial purchase
Planning efficiency	Accuracy of budgets/schedules v actual costs/lead times
Competitor comparison	Comparing key criteria (timeliness, reliability, price, service profile) against competitor performance
Cost ratio rating	Cost incurred by the buyer as a result of particular types of supply failure. (Eg 'every time the supplier delivers Component X a day late, the cost to us is £x')

Learning Objective 3.0: Measuring the performance of the buyer

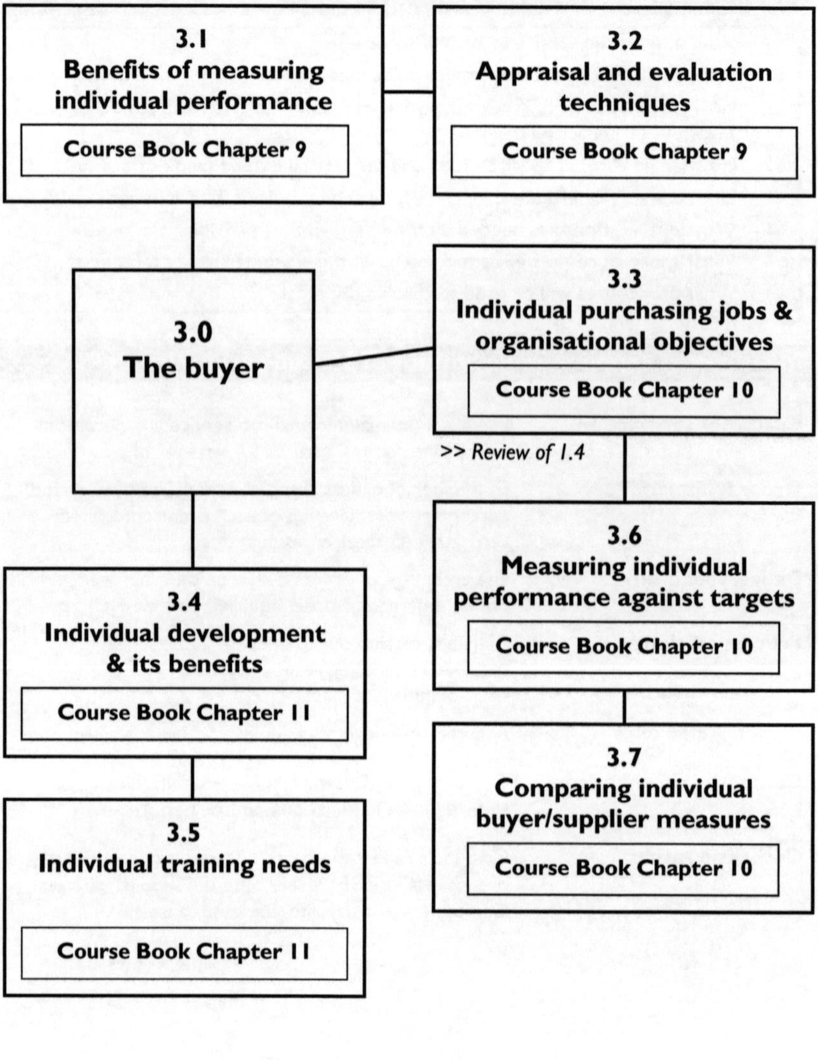

Define and explain the benefits of a well managed and structured approach to measuring an individual's performance 3.1

Performance appraisal is 'the regular and systematic review of performance and assessment of potential, with the aim of producing action programmes to develop both work and individuals'.

Purposes of individual performance measurement

- ❑ Develop a consensus between individual, functional corporate objectives
- ❑ Enable comparison of actual with target results > improvement planning
- ❑ Generate/exchange feedback on performance > learning, motivation, improvement
- ❑ Identify and resolve reasons for sub-standard performance (individual and systemic)
- ❑ Provide performance-related basis for merit pay awards and salary review
- ❑ Identify individual training and development needs > plan and evaluate interventions
- ❑ Identify individual potential for career development > career/succession planning

Benefits of a well-managed and structured approach

For the organisation:

- ☑ Supports human resource planning (HRP): skill availability/gaps, flexibility etc
- ☑ Supports evaluation of recruitment and selection processes
- ☑ Supports reward management: relevant, objective performance-related criteria
- ☑ Compliance with relevant law and regulation (eg fair selection for redundancy)
- ☑ Needs- and improvements-focused approach to development planning ***[>> Unit 3.4]***
- ☑ Requires managers to form coherent, complete and objective view of individual's performance *and* to offer regular, specific, development-focused feedback >>
  - ☑ Enhanced performance management/improvement
  - ☑ Enhanced manager-employee communication/relations
  - ☑ Basis for continuous learning, improvement, innovation and empowerment
- ☑ Helps to identify (and increase visibility of) purchasing contribution

For the individual:

- ☑ Clear goals, targets and standards: know what expected to achieve, how contribute
- ☑ Regular, relevant feedback: supports learning and motivation
- ☑ Fair basis for comparison with others (eg re bonuses, fast-track development)
- ☑ Opportunity to discuss work problems and training/development needs
- ☑ Support for training/development and performance improvements ***[>> Unit 3.4]***

3.1 Define and explain the benefits of a well managed and structured approach to measuring an individual's performance

Investors in People (IiP)

The **Investors in People** scheme provides a national benchmark standard for investment in employee training and development. Organisations seeking accreditation under the scheme must audit their current training practice and provision and bring them into line with published standards.

Principles	***Key indicators (relevant to performance appraisal)***
Developing strategies to improve the performance of the organisation	• A strategy for improving the performance of the organisation is clearly defined and understood • Learning and development is planned to achieve the organisation's objectives
Taking action to improve the performance of the organisation	• Managers are effective in leading, managing and developing people • People's contribution to the organisation is recognised and valued • People learn and develop effectively
Evaluating the impact on the performance of the organisation	• Investment in people improves the performance of the organisation • Improvements are continually made to the way people are managed and developed

☑ Opportunity to review current policies and practices against a recognised benchmark

☑ Framework for planning future strategy and action

☑ Structured way to improve the effectiveness of training and development activities

Explain how appraisal and evaluation techniques can be employed to measure and improve performance 3.2

Informal performance evaluation and feedback

Managers should be constantly **monitoring performance** of individuals:

- Requiring reports on key results, deviations from plan (reporting by exception)
- Observing and listening to the flow of work and relationships
- Sampling individual outputs

And giving **performance feedback**:

- *Motivational feedback* (prasie, encouragement): acknowledge, reward and encourage positive behaviour/performance > boost confidence.
- *Developmental feedback* (constructive criticism, coaching, counselling): identify performance problems/weaknesses and plan for improvement> increase competence.

☒ Managers may obtain random, subjective, partial impression of individual performance
☒ Focus on weaknesses, errors: less attention to proactive development
☒ Different criteria and standards of objectivity > undermines credibility
☒ Managers may not give adequate feedback to individuals

Formal appraisal systems

- ❑ Identification of criteria for assessment and specific performance measures
- ❑ Report giving assessment and feedback in relation to criteria
- ❑ Interview for verbal feedback, problem-solving, improvement planning
- ❑ Provision for review of (or appeal against) appraisal, if required
- ❑ Preparation and agreement of improvement/development action plans
- ❑ Implementation and follow-up monitoring of progress
- ❑ Usually on an annual or six-monthly cycle

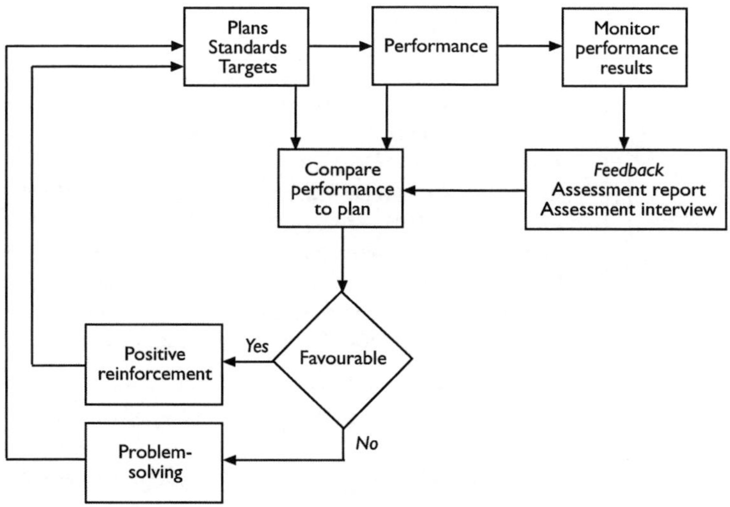

3.2 Explain how appraisal and evaluation techniques can be employed to measure and improve performance

Appraisal procedures

Frequency	• **Continual/ongoing**: informal monitoring and review plus checkpoints or milestone measurements and feedback meetings. (Useful for tight control eg project work; where requirements changeable; where manager and team in close contact) • **Periodic reviews**: series of scheduled appraisals at quarterly or six-monthly intervals. (Benefits of structured approach, but at greater frequency where tighter control required) • **Annual appraisal**. (Often perceived as negative, retrospective, wasteful of opportunities for improvement/adjustment)
Appraiser/ source of feedback *(Involving* ***stakeholders*** *in buyer's performance)*	• **Line manager appraisal**: detailed knowledge of task requirement, opportunity to manage performance *but* may be liable to bias, may affect working relationship. • **Self-assessment**: useful element of appraisal, encourages 'ownership' of improvement needs/goals. Standard form: o Key tasks and objectives o Assessment of progress/attainment of each o Perceived strengths/weaknesses, training/development needs o Performance and career aspirations for following period • **Peer appraisal**: feedback on interpersonal criteria eg ability to work with others *but* subject to reluctance, bias • **Upward appraisal**: feedback on leadership style and skills *but* subject to fear of retribution • **Internal customer appraisal**: feedback on P & S service • **Appraisal by suppliers**: feedback on negotiating, contract/ relationship management skills etc. *but* subject to reluctance • **360-degree (multi-source) feedback:** multiple sources > rounded view, reduced bias, increased stakeholder involvement
Appraisal techniques	• **Overall or guided assessment**: comments on attributes • **Grading/rating scales:** selection of level/degree to which attributes demonstrated ('good/fair/poor', points, graphic scale) • **Behavioural incident**: measure behaviour against 'typical' behaviour, as defined by critical incidents/examples • **Results oriented**: eg review against specific agreed targets/standards, management by objectives ***[>> Unit 3.3]*** • **Assessment centres**: group appraisal exercises, interviews, role plays etc (often used for managerial jobs not easy to measure in terms of outputs)

Explain how appraisal and evaluation techniques can be employed to measure and improve performance — 3.2

Performance measures
[>> *Unit 3.6*]

Criteria for individual performance appraisal should be:

- ❑ Capable of being measured reliably and consistently
- ❑ Capable of differentiating/comparing individuals
- ❑ Within the individual's power (to learn, improve)
- ❑ Acceptable to individuals as fair and relevant

Quantitative criteria: focus on efficiency and productivity levels and improvements eg purchase orders per period, cycle time, error rates, on-time-in-full delivery. (Used where purchasing roles primarily clerical/administrative.)

Qualitative criteria: focus on purchasing knowledge/skills, teamworking, service, contribution to quality/supplier relationships etc. (Used in more relational, strategic purchasing roles.)

Appraisal interviews

(Maier)

- **Tell and sell:** manager gives assessment, then tries to gain acceptance of improvement plan
- **Tell and listen**: manager gives assessment, then invites response > problem solving and improvement planning
- **Problem-solving**: manager acts as facilitator and coach > collaborative identification of work problems, potential and aspirations > explore solutions and options. (Potentially positive, motivating, innovative *but* requires strong interpersonal skills!)

Improving individual appraisal

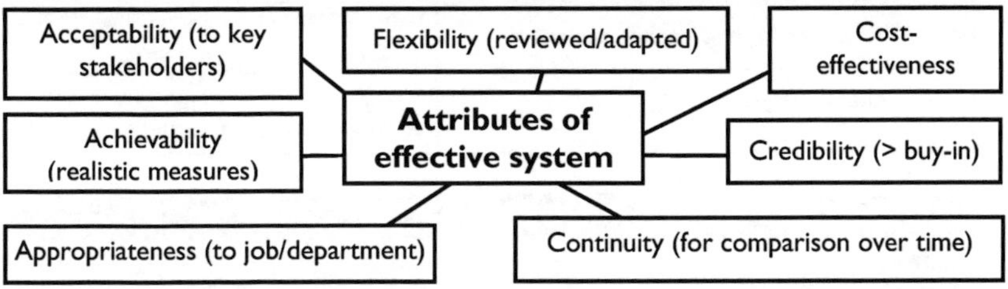

(Lysons & Farrington)

Common problems with appraisal:

- ❑ Poorly perceived *(Lockwood)* as form-filling exercise (bureaucracy), vague discussion (chat), one-sided process (judgement) or excuse to address conflicts (confrontation)
- ❑ Low priority > inadequate preparation, unconstructive orientation
- ❑ Appraisal criteria not clearly related to organisational goals or stakeholder needs
- ❑ Employees treated unfairly, or alienated, by eg breach of confidentiality, bias, failure to listen, lack of objective performance measurement data, unachievable targets
- ❑ Opportunity for 'blame culture' > adversarial and defensive process
- ❑ Changes to targets and priorities > criteria irrelevant, outdated
- ❑ Little or no action taken to follow up appraisal (eg with rewards, training)

3.2 Explain how appraisal and evaluation techniques can be employed to measure and improve performance

Appraising the appraisal system

Monitoring/evaluation method	Criteria evaluated
Asking appraisers and appraisees how they felt about the process, using: • attitude surveys • appraisal interviews and discussions	Is the system perceived to be fair? Worthwhile? Taken seriously? Are appraisers able to be honest/constructive? Do appraisees feel threatened/judged? Supported/heard/involved? What additional resources are needed?
Monitoring selected performance indicators	Has problem-solving been implemented? Has performance improved?
Monitoring training programmes	Have training needs been identified? Has training been planned and implemented?
Monitoring promotions and managerial succession	Have promotable individuals been identified? Have development opportunities been identified and implemented?
Monitoring other HR indicators, eg: • staff turnover and absenteeism • disciplinary and grievance actions	Has appraisal had a positive or negative effect on manager/team relations? On team morale and motivation?
Cost-benefit analysis	Is appraisal worthwhile? Efficiently conducted? Cost-effective?

Performance management

Performance management is an approach that 'focuses on future performance planning and improvement rather than retrospective appraisal. It provides the basis for regular and frequent dialogues between managers and individuals/teams about performance and development needs.'

- ❑ Preparation of performance agreements/contracts: objectives, performance measures and required competencies
- ❑ Preparation of performance and development plans: identified performance and personal development needs in order for agreements to be met
- ❑ Management of performance through the year: feedback, reviews and problem solving
- ❑ Annual performance review: assessing progress and agreeing future plans.

Analyse and explain how individual components of a purchasing role link to the overall objectives of the organisation 3.3

Purchasing roles and organisational objectives

Organisational objectives

↓

Functional (P & S) objectives

↓

INDIVIDUAL/TEAM OBJECTIVES

Cascade of objectives
[>> Unit 1.4]

Output/improvement targets	Increase orders processed by 3% by [date] Maintain inventory levels at no more than £x
Performance standards	Process 90% of customer orders within 24 hours
	Proposals for materials specifications are fully supported by relevant data and justified by return-on-investment analysis
Projects to be completed	E-procurement system to be operational by [date]
Standing objectives	Ethical guidelines for purchasing upheld at all times
Development objectives	Participate effectively in negotiating team (measured by ability to ....) by [date]

Management by objectives (MbO)

Management by objectives is a systematic approach to integrating individual, functional and corporate plans, as part of an ongoing programme of goal-setting and performance review for all levels of management.

Develop clear strategic objectives
↓
Define individual areas of responsibility
↓
Define key tasks to achieve objectives
↓
Define key results to achieve key tasks and methods of monitoring/measuring
↓
Agree improvement action plans
↓
Monitor and review at agreed intervals

- ☑ Clarifies organisational/unit goals
- ☑ Focuses attention on priority areas
- ☑ Systematically converts strategic plans > co-ordinated action plans, budgets
- ☑ Involves individuals > commitment to defined targets, accountabilities
- ☑ Supplies systematic info for planning and control, individual appraisal and performance management

- ☒ Danger of rigidity from complex planning
- ☒ Employee relations problems if staff perceive added accountability without resources or empowerment
- ☒ May require significant change in structure, culture, management style

Individual contribution to profitability, workload management, development of purchasing infrastructure & competency ***[>> Unit 1.4]***

3.3 Analyse and explain how individual components of a purchasing role link to the overall objectives of the organisation

Setting individual objectives

Effective objectives:

☑ Promote unity of direction, co-ordination and efficient organisation
☑ Enable limited resources to be optimally allocated
☑ Support objective performance measurement and accountability
☑ Support flexibility by focusing on critical success factors rather than inputs (which may change) and processes (which may cause a bureaucratic/inward focus)
☑ Enable tasks to be broken down into manageable, time-bounded chunks
☑ Support individual learning, motivation and change

***S**pecific*	Stating precisely what desired outcomes or deliverables are
***M**easurable*	Susceptible to monitoring, review and measurement
***A**ttainable*	Realistically achievable, using capacities, capabilities, resources available
***R**elevant*	Directly linked to strategic and functional success factors
***T**ime-bound*	Including target deadlines for completion (or review)
***E**valuated*	Considered worthwhile, on the basis of cost/benefit analysis
***R**esponsible*	Taking into account potential impacts on key stakeholders (and formulated with their participation/agreement if possible)

eg

Key task:	Improve efficiency/productivity in purchase ordering
Objective:	Increase productivity of purchase order generation by 5%
Performance measures:	Purchase orders per employee Cost per purchase order Hours required to complete requisition & purchase order % of purchase orders communicated electronically
Timescale:	December 200X: review monthly

Problems with objective-setting

- Constantly changing focus/targets
- Inadequate info for measuring performance
- Too few/too many objectives
- Poorly constructed (un-SMART) objectives
- Insufficiently challenging objectives
- Limited range of objectives
- Rigid objectives

Analyse and explain how an individual's knowledge, expertise and skills can be developed to individual/organisational benefit 3.4

Why develop people?

For trainees:

☑ Enhanced skills/competence > self-esteem, achievement and reward potential

☑ Opportunities for career development and potentially job satisfaction

☑ Opportunities for personal development, enhanced employability

For the organisation:

☑ Enhanced skills/competence/ethics > better performance, commitment, contribution

☑ Enhanced versatility and flexibility > more efficient utilisation, adaptability to change

☑ Reduced accidents, errors/wastage and other consequences of poor performance

☑ Less need for supervision, freeing management for proactive roles (or delayering)

☑ Enhanced employer brand (eg as Investors in People) to attract quality labour

☑ Support for continuous learning, innovation, improvement > competitive advantage

Benefits of a well-managed and systematic approach:

☑ Compliance with employment legislation/regulation (equal opportunity, health and safety, employment protection, employee involvement etc)

☑ Support for ethical values eg fairness and equity in dealing with people

☑ Communicates/reinforces culture: desired values/behaviours

☑ Enables organisation to meet its current/forecast HR needs via sourcing (from outside) and development/retention (from inside)

☑ Supports motivation, commitment and retention of skilled labour, by:

- Offering opportunities for recognition and reward (via appraisal)
- Offering job satisfaction (via job design, training and development)
- Showing value/consideration for employee needs and hygiene issues (via health, safety and welfare, diversity policy, employee involvement) etc.

☑ Improves organisational performance of individuals, teams and the organisation as a whole, by:

- Acquiring or developing high-calibre, job-relevant skills/competencies
- Ensuring that employees are informed and empowered to pursue objectives
- Encouraging labour flexibility and versatility for innovation and change
- Facilitating continuous organisational learning and development

3.4 Analyse and explain how an individual's knowledge, expertise and skills can be developed to individual/organisational benefit

Systematic approach to training

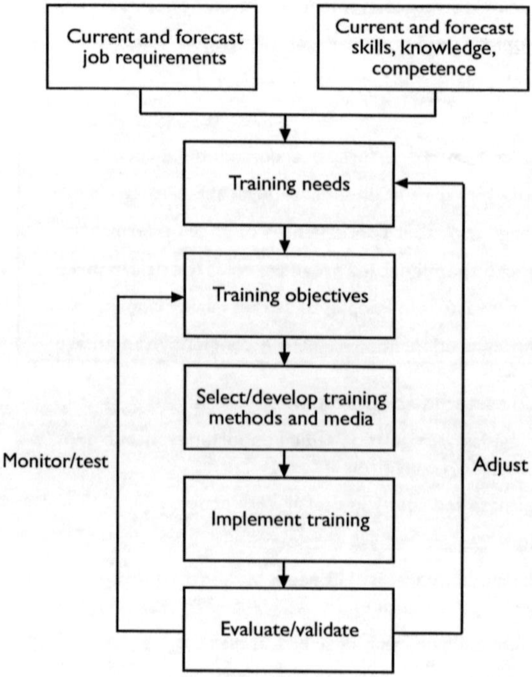

Formal **training needs analysis** *[>> Unit 3.5]*

Training **methods/media:**

- *On-the-job:* job instruction, coaching, job rotation, assistant positions, projects
- *Off-the-job:* classes, case studies, role plays, distance learning, site visits, computer-based and e-learning, blended learning, action learning
- *Informal:* self-reflection, opportunistic coaching by manager, feedback etc.

Training may be **evaluated** for: trainee satisfaction, learning outcomes, job performance, and wider impacts (eg on results, culture).

Training methods and media

Methods	Advantages	Disadvantages
On-the-job methods		
Sitting with Nellie	Learning in context Immediate feedback/adjustment Establishes relationships + skills	Only as effective as 'Nellie' Transfers work culture (not always best practice)
Coaching	Flexible to trainee pace/needs Involves trainee in problem-solving Learning connected to job context	Requires coaching skills
Mentoring	Flexibly adjusted to trainee needs Encourages self-development Longer-term, wider development	Requires mentoring time and skills
Rotating/shadowing	Trainees experience responsibility with controlled risk May increase job satisfaction Aids management succession	May be perceived as not 'real' work May be perceived as 'nuisance' by full-timers

Analyse and explain how an individual's knowledge, expertise and skills can be developed to individual/organisational benefit 3.4

Methods	Advantages	Disadvantages
Off-the-job methods		
Lectures/taught classes	Suits theorist/reflector styles and theory/principle-based subjects Suits large numbers of trainees	Doesn't suit hands-on Difficult learning passively Relative inflexibility
Case studies, role plays, simulations	Experimentation without risk Active problem-solving, participation	May not transfer to real job Euphoria of training may cause anticlimax at work
Open/distance learning	Economical, especially, where trainees geographically dispersed Flexible for learner pace, needs, circumstances	Only as effective as materials/programme May not suit activists/pragmatists
Visits and tours	Aids generalisation/application Raises awareness of big picture	Limited depth of content Limited flexibility
E-learning	Economical where hardware/software available Flexible to trainee pace, needs Standardised training	Technology may alienate non-expert users May not transfer to real job context

Training and development

Training is 'a planned process to modify attitude, knowledge or skill behaviour through learning experiences, to achieve effective performance in any activity or range of activities' *(Manpower Services Commission)*

Development is the wider process of 'achieving outstanding organisational performance through empowering people to achieve and give of their best'.

Development includes activities for:

- Gaining experience of different levels/functions/sites
- Receiving guidance, support and counselling to formulate personal/career goals
- Gaining access to learning experiences to develop skills and knowledge
- Facilitating career planning and management succession within the organisation
- Continuously updating professional skills/knowledge/standards (CPD)

Evaluating training and development activity *(Kirkpatrick)*

Level	*Measurement*
1 Trainee reaction	Feedback forms, attitude surveys: was training satisfying/useful etc?
2 Learning	Post-training observation, testing: did training meet objectives?
3 Job behaviour	Observation, work sampling: has learning been transferred to job?
4 Performance	Performance measures: did training impact on results, culture etc?

3.5 Evaluate and explain the use of a range of techniques to analyse the training needs of individual buyers

- **FOCUSED training** (effective): employees are trained only in directly job-relevant skills, in which they have an identified skill/knowledge gap (as a result of systematic training needs analysis).
- **UNFOCUSED training** (often ineffective): training arises as a result of *ad hoc* requests by employees or managers, trainer marketing or blanket training policies.

Emerging training needs

- ❑ Changes in legislation, technology or work methods > gap in current performance
- ❑ Critical incidents (problems/events which affect a key task) identified by individual, manager or third-party stakeholders > identified need for training/improvement
- ❑ Developmental discussions (performance appraisal, coaching, mentoring) > identify scope for improvement, development aspirations
- ❑ Self-assessment and personal development activities > identify potential for growth

But does not necessarily take account of organisational/future skill requirements…

Systematic training needs analysis

Measure what staff need to be able to do:
- Job/role/competence analysis
- Job descriptions, job profiles
- Future plans of organisation/unit

Measure what staff can do:
- Observation, work sampling
- Self-assessment, attitude surveys
- Formal appraisal, feedback

Identify 'gap' as potential need for training/learning:
- What other interventions (eg counselling, discipline, problem-solving) may be more appropriate?
- What type of training would be most appropriate for this skill gap and these trainees?

1. Decide on method of analysis to be used (self-assessment, interview, testing etc)
2. Define required level of competence for the job > benchmark standards
3. Measure present level of competence, using agreed methods
4. Compare present competence with benchmark > identify knowledge/skill gaps
5. Design and implement interventions (including training) to remedy gaps
6. Monitor, review and feed back on progress as appropriate

@ ***Functional level:*** eg on restructuring, change of policy, new systems
@ ***Job level:*** eg groups of new staff, new jobs created, or updating of job descriptions
@ ***Individual level:*** ongoing appraisal, feedback, improvement/development planning

Evaluate and explain the use of a range of techniques to analyse the training needs of individual buyers 3.5

Determining competence requirements

- ☐ **Job analysis**: systematic analysis of characteristics and requirements of a job (using observation, documentary evidence, interviews, questionnaires, diary-keeping etc)

- ☐ **Job description:** a broad statement of the purpose, scope, duties and responsibilities of a particular job (as determined by job analysis).

JOB DESCRIPTION	
Job title and unit/department *Job summary* (function, position in structure) *Job content* (main tasks) *Key accountabilities* *Reporting and collaborative relationships* *Working conditions* *Employment conditions*	☑ Use for TNA: define job requirements and potential problem areas ☒ Only able to give accurate/meaningful description of simple, repetitive jobs ☒ If rigidly adhered to > demarcation disputes, loss of flexibility

- ☐ **Job profiles** (job specifications)**:** translate job descriptions into a statement of skills and abilities needed to perform the job competently (like **person specifications** used in selection and appraisal: describe 'ideal job holder')

JOB PROFILE	
Knowledge, skills and abilities *Educational attainments/qualifications* *Occupational/vocational training* *Professional certification* *Types and levels of work experience*	☑ Handy checklist of needs for education, training, certification, development experience etc

- ☐ **Competence analysis and definition:** profiles based on key success factors in a given business or sector, offering a more flexible menu-driven alternative.

COMPETENCE DEFINITION	
Key roles (units of competence) *Specific activities (elements of competence)* *To what standard (performance criteria)* *In what contexts (range statement)* *Underpinning knowledge and understanding*	☑ Direct link to strategic objectives and best practice in occupation ☑ Readily adaptable to changing needs (non-prescriptive about job specifics) ☑ Applicable at all levels of organisation > consistent values and practices

Measuring current competence

Performance measures ***[>> Unit 3.6]***

Appraisals ***[>> Unit 3.2]***

3.6 Explain how to measure individual performance against pre-set targets

Information for performance measurement

Data are the raw materials (facts and figures) which become **information** once they have been processed so as to have meaning for a user.

Good quality information for performance measurement:

☑ **Relates** to the criteria being measured: data supports evaluation of specific performance indicators (and does not contain irrelevant data)

☑ **Relevant** to the needs of the individual and manager: focus on key tasks and performance indicators; elicits info on both strengths and weaknesses; addresses areas within individual's power to change

☑ **Accurate** within user's needs: factually correct but not too detailed for use

☑ **Valid** (shows what it purports to show) + **consistent** (means same thing from one individual to another and over time) + **comparable** (allows meaningful comparison between individuals and over time) = **fair**

☑ **Timely**: data is available (and up-to-date) within time period which makes it useful

☑ **Appropriately communicated**: usable format and medium

☑ **Cost-effective**: value outweighs gathering/processing costs

Information requirements include:

❑ **Ongoing performance data** from operational information and reporting systems (P & S and other functions), observation and output sampling, re:

- Transactional activity (eg requisitions issued, orders placed, invoices cleared etc)
- Budgetary conformance (eg actual expenditure or stock requirements v estimate)
- Operational performance (eg cost savings, inventory levels, contract management)
- Strategic contribution (eg margin improvement, supply base rationalisation)

NB: clear argument for ***integration*** *of information systems across business (and even supply chain) > support supply chain performance measurement.*

❑ **Bespoke performance information** for which a specific data search, research or report may be required. Eg:

- Performance audit and progress/completion report on a purchasing project
- Report on the progress or results of purchasing initiatives (eg overseas sourcing)
- Feedback and review of staff training/development programmes

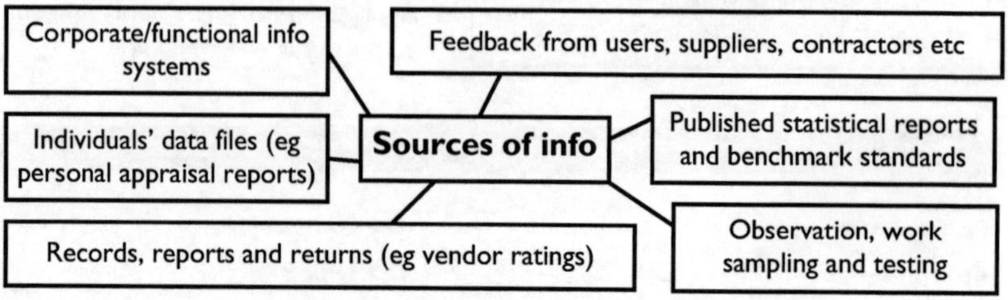

Explain how to measure individual performance against pre-set targets — 3.6

Individual performance measures for purchasing roles

- **External**: eg internal customer satisfaction, external customer satisfaction, number/type of quality/delivery complaints
- **Operational**: eg on-time/in-full deliveries, number/type of transaction errors, productivity
- **Financial measures**: eg costs and cost reductions, financial ratio improvements
- **Develop measures**: eg number of suggestions/improvements made, training hours, involvement in quality teams etc.

Statistical performance measures (metrics)	**eg**
Cost efficiency	Annual cost savings or margin contribution Prices negotiated/paid v standard prices or market indices Prices negotiated/paid v budget
Productivity	Purchase orders/material receipts completed per employee Cost per purchase order/receipt
Technology	% of automatic (v manual) transactions
Productivity	Hours required to complete a requisition and purchase order Average lead time (from requisition to receipt)
Supplier leverage	Number of suppliers per £x of spend % of purchases made from preferred suppliers
Quality	% of transactions requiring correction after process
Customer satisfaction	% of deliveries received in full on time (IFOT) from major suppliers Number of complaints/queries received from users/customers
Inventory	% inventory reduction Number of product stockouts and emergency orders Comparison of actual stock with target stock
Compliance	% of ethical/environmental targets met
Projects	% of milestones met with full conformance, on schedule % of deliverables achieved to stakeholder satisfaction

NB: also **qualitative measures** eg:

- Effective contribution to cross-functional teamworking
- Internal/external customer (or project stakeholder) satisfaction
- Personal and skill development
- Contribution to particular initiatives or goals (eg quality or service improvements, make or buy decisions, outsourcing management, innovation, supplier development)
- Effectiveness of supplier/customer relationship management
- Understanding of (and contribution to) organisational objectives

3.7 Compare the relevant performance measures of the buyer with those of his/her respective suppliers

Stakeholders in the buyer's performance

Stakeholders are individuals and groups who have an interest or 'stake' in a process or outcome (such as performance measurement and management).

Stakeholders in buyer performance

- Owners/sponsors of activity: line or project manager. *Key interest:* achievement of objectives, contribution to success factors. *Role:* main input to appraisal.
- Secondary stakeholders eg suppliers' labour pool; interest groups; consumers. *Key interest:* ethical, socially responsible practices; environmental responsibility; consumer protection. *Role:* indirect 'voice' > criteria.
- Internal customers and users. *Key interest:* provision of Five Rights, added value, knowledge, co-operation etc. *Role:* should input to criteria and appraisal.
- Suppliers, contractors and outsourced service providers. *Key interest:* fair treatment/payment, sustainable business relationship, value sharing. *Role:* may input to appraisal

Comparing buyer and supplier performance measures

Different performance measures?	• Key measures of buyer performance: indicators of skills and knowledge, efficiency, effectiveness, contribution to goals/targets of P & S function and organisation as a whole. • Key measures of supplier performance: 10 Cs **[>> *Unit 2.4*]** (*NB* tend to be organisational rather than individual) ***BUT***: • Competence, capacity, commitment to quality, consistency, cleanliness, compliance etc can also be seen as KPIs for buyers • Both sets of measures contribute to *buying organisation's* goals
Reciprocal expectations	Buyers measure supplier performance: suppliers also measure buyer performance! (Suppliers prioritise 'good' customers by offering priority levels of service, willingness to partner, flexibility for urgent demands, price discounts etc.) *[See next page]*
Conflicting expectations?	Supplier measures of a buyer's performance may (or may not) conflict with buying organisation's measurement. • Adversarial buyer-supplier relationships: buyer performance (lowest price, maximum risk transfer, maximum share of value gains) at *expense* of supplier (measures buyer on fairness, risk/gain sharing etc) • Collaborative buyer-supplier relationships: buyer/supplier performance aimed at collaboration, supply continuity, mutual commitment, maximising value gains > mutual benefit.

Compare the relevant performance measures of the buyer with those of his/her respective suppliers 3.7

Suppliers' performance measurements for buyers

Operational:

- Fair, transparent, efficient quotation/tender process
- Efficient, fair contract negotiation and management
- Quality of info and communication
- Prompt, fair payment of invoices
- Accessibility in event of queries/problems
- Constructive handling of conflicts/disputes
- Collaboration on reverse logistics
- Ethical conduct
- Fair sharing of risks and rewards of added value, innovation etc

Added value:

- Willingness to work with supplier to create and share value gains
- Willingness to consult supplier when developing specifications
- Willingness to share knowledge and expertise (eg reciprocal training) and info (eg cost transparency) to develop supplier
- Responsiveness to supplier recommendations
- 'Intelligent customer' qualities (product knowledge, supply market knowledge, ability to specify effectively, procurement efficiency)

Reciprocal satisfaction measures *(Neely, Adams & Kennerley)*

Supplier satisfaction measures: *What do our suppliers want and need from us?*	**Supplier contribution measures:** *What do we want and need from our suppliers?*
• Supplier satisfaction level • Average spend per supplier trend • Average supplier retention (length of service) • % value purchased through single-source supplier arrangements • % suppliers to whom demand visibility provided • Level of demand forecast accuracy • Level of specification changes • Level of supplier payments overdue • Level of supplier billing errors	• Contribution to revenues/cost savings • Complaints about supplier performance • Level of product quality non-conformance • Level of late delivery (to promise/request) • Level of after-sales product/service problems • Level of customer warranty/liability claims attributed to supplier failure • Level of supplier-generated improvement suggestions contributed/implemented • Perceived value for money of supplier contribution